T0001543

PRESSURE CANNING FOR BEGINNERS

PRESSURE CANNING
FOR BEGINNERS

A STEP-BY-STEP GUIDE WITH 50 RECIPES

Amber Benson

ROCKRIDGE
PRESS

As of press time, the URLs in this book link or refer to existing websites on the internet. Rockridge Press is not responsible for the outdated, inaccurate, or incomplete content available on these sites.

Copyright © 2023 by Rockridge Press

All rights reserved. No part of this publication may be reproduced, stored in a retrieval system, or transmitted in any form or by any means, electronic, mechanical, photocopying, recording, scanning, or otherwise, without the prior written permission of the Publisher. Requests to the Publisher for permission should be addressed to the Permissions Department, Rockridge Press, 1955 Broadway, Suite 400, Oakland, CA 94612.

First Rockridge Press trade paperback edition 2023

Rockridge Press and the Rockridge Press logo are trademarks or registered trademarks of Callisto Media Inc. and/or its affiliates in the United States and other countries and may not be used without written permission.

For general information on our other products and services, please contact our Customer Care Department within the United States at (866) 744-2665, or outside the United States at (510) 253-0500.

Paperback ISBN: 978-1-63878-000-7 | eBook ISBN: 978-1-63807-628-5

Manufactured in the United States of America

Interior and Cover Designer: Karmen Lizzul
Art Producer: Hannah Dickerson
Editor: Marjorie DeWitt
Production Editor: Emily Sheehan
Production Manager: Lanore Coloprisco

Photography by Darren Muir: cover, ii, v, x; © Andrew Purcell: ix; © Marija Vidal: 44, 90, back cover center; © Nadine Greeff/Stocksy: 22, back cover left; © Cavan Images/Alamy Stock Photo: 66; © Davide Illini/Stocksy: 112, back cover right. Food styling by Yolanda Muir: cover. Illustrations © Amber Day

Author photo by Julia Mina Photography

10 9 8 7 6 5 4 3 2 1 0

For Daddio.

CONTENTS

INTRODUCTION

This book is something I've been working on for eighteen years through my work with food and restaurants. It all started when I was living in northwest Missouri and I begged a friend to teach me how to can. Shortly thereafter, I moved to Northern California, where I worked on an organic pear and cherry farm opening a restaurant. I had big plans to create and sell jams, jellies, and other goods we harvested from the farm. During that time, regulatory authorities had not yet written food safety codes to validate commercial canning for restaurant use, and a simple variance was how you could get approval to sell these items. I decided I needed to become an expert, so I started doing some research. I came across the University of California Cooperative Extension, which invited me to apply and eventually join their Master Food Preserver certification program. The education and certification allowed me to pursue volunteer opportunities all over Northern California, where I got to teach classes, participate in workshops, travel, complete continuing education courses, and study all forms of food preservation from a research-based, scientific approach with a focus on how to safely preserve foods. I have now been certified and teaching all forms of food preservation for more than six years.

I love pressure canning because it is a scientifically proven way to safely preserve food. Pressure canning can sound intimidating if you've never done it before, but by following a few simple and clear guidelines, it becomes approachable and fun! With a small investment in a pressure canner and yearly routine maintenance to ensure your equipment is working properly, you can be pressure canning for years to come.

I always dreamed of having a beautifully stocked pantry full of food I created. Pressure canning gives me the freedom and control to do so. I love that pressure canning allows me to get creative in the kitchen, reduce waste by using excess ingredients or an abundant garden harvest, and efficiently create batches of food that will stay safe in my pantry for a year, providing me with quick, go-to meals to feed many or a few.

I will take you through the mechanics of pressure canning in this step-by-step introduction so you feel confident in your own kitchen. I will teach you how to safely preserve foods in exciting and delicious recipes designed specifically to teach you how to start pressure canning at home!

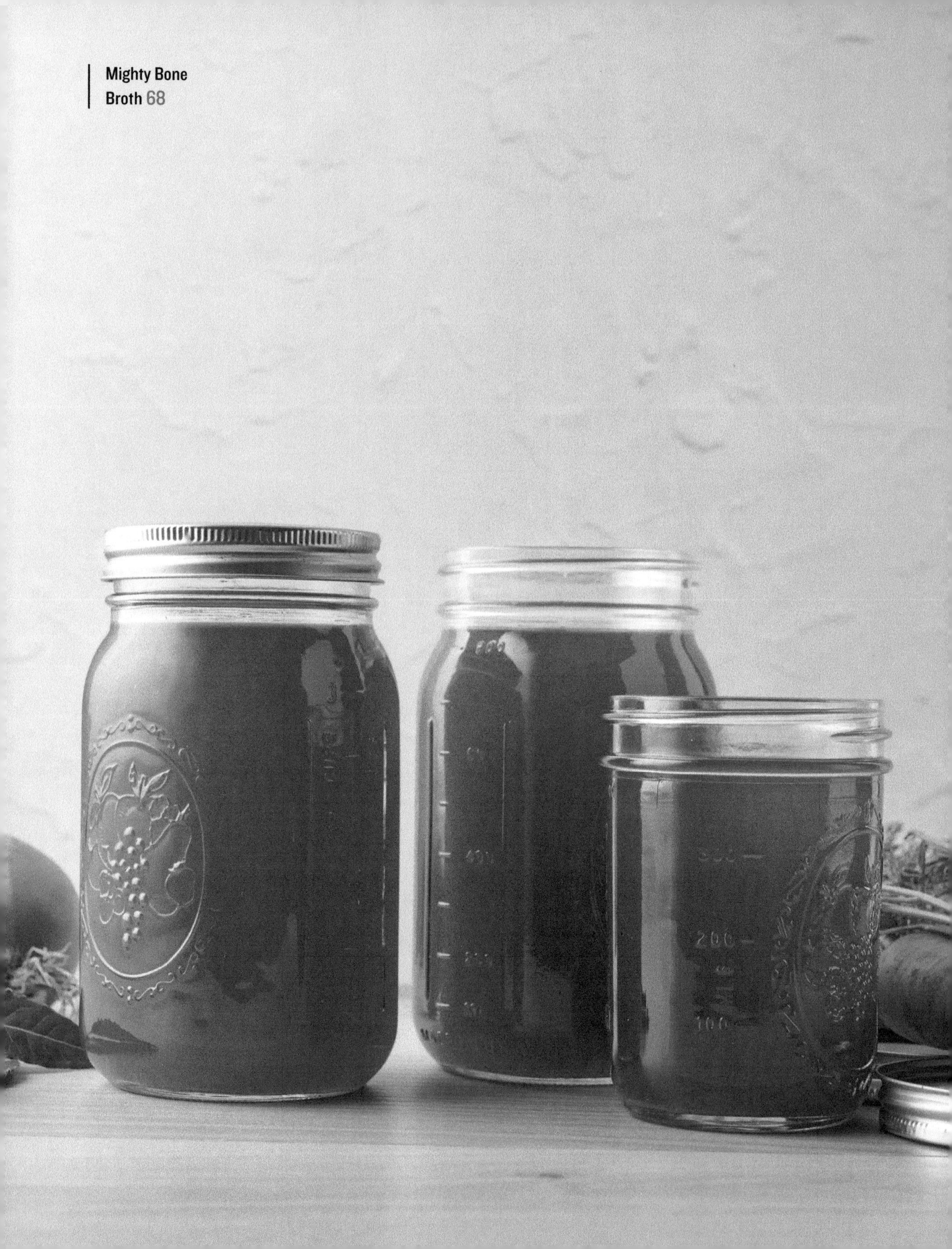

Mighty Bone Broth 68

CHAPTER 1

Getting Started with Pressure Canning

Welcome to pressure canning for beginners! This first chapter will cover how to get started with pressure canning. I will walk you through the magic of canning and the pressure canning fundamentals and explore common questions and answers around pressure canning. I will discuss safety while canning, allay fears around botulism, teach you how to stock your kitchen, and introduce the necessary tools and equipment to successfully pressure can at home. I will also provide you with a pressure canning step-by-step guide that you can refer to as you work your way through the recipes.

The Magic of Canning Your Food

Learning the art, science, and magic of preserving food through pressure canning opens up a world of possibility. Preservation, by definition, means to maintain something. To maintain something means to provide necessities for life or continued existence. Pressure canning gives you control over many aspects of your kitchen and food that you cannot get through other methods of preservation. The magic of canning as a food preservation tool allows you to extend the life of food, drives convenience, helps save money by reducing food waste, and brings a sense of control into your kitchen. Having a large pantry of preserved goods is not only something to brag about but also quite a beautiful sight. If you have practiced other methods of preservation, such as dehydrating, freezing, or water bath canning, you might be familiar with pressure canning.

Extend the life of your food: This means that the large Sunday morning farmers' market haul or garden harvest does not go to waste. Pressure canning gives you the tools to preserve that bounty far beyond the few days it would otherwise last. Did summer gardens leave you with more zucchini than your neighbors care to eat? Do you have leftover bits of spring onions and trimmings of potatoes from a weeknight meal? Save those bits to simmer up a pot of savory stew that will nourish your loved ones months later or provide a healthy sipping broth for a busy morning on the go.

Affordable and convenient meals: Find a great deal on ground beef at the market? Double or triple a recipe for Taco Tuesday, and now you've got a pantry that can support you on evenings when you need dinner ready, *fast*. Pressure canning creates the convenience of jump-starting meals at the end of a long day.

Reduce food waste: Have you ever planned a meal that required a special ingredient that the market only sold in bulk and were faced with how to use up the remainder of that ingredient? This is where pressure canning shines! Pressure canning provides a yearlong shelf life for your delicious creations. As I cook throughout the week or plan special meals, I consider what I can save or batch to create something I will use in the future. For example, if you decide to make lasagna and know you will have an extraordinary number of leftover tomatoes from the can or your garden, you could plan to can a batch of homemade barbecue sauce to keep on the shelf until your next grilling adventure.

Pressure Canning 101

Pressure canning is a way of preserving food to make it shelf stable. This is beneficial because it saves you money, time, and energy and controls the quality and ingredients of your food. Pressure canning, as opposed to other methods of canning, allows you to safely preserve foods lower in acidity, like meats and vegetables. This possibility provides the freedom to get creative with different foods and ingredient combinations.

Pressure canning uses water to create steam pressure that heats to a much higher temperature than water bath canning. This steam pressure process creates a vacuum that seals the jars, and the higher temperatures control for food safety. The food safety basics that we control are time, temperature, and oxygen.

By choosing to pressure can, you can also control for food acidity by selecting a canning method that we know is compatible for most types of food. With its simple canning steps, pressure canning eliminates food safety concerns such as botulism, mold, oxygen, and bacteria. I'm here to assure you that you are more than capable of safely pressure canning!

ACIDITY AND PH

I have referred to pressure canning as a great way to safely preserve low-acid foods, but what does that mean? Acidity in foods is important when it comes to food preservation, and we determine that by measuring acidity and alkalinity on the pH scale; pH represents an ingredient's potential for hydrogen, as ingredients with more hydrogen ions present are naturally more acidic. The pH scale ranges from 0 to 14, with 7 being neutral. Counterintuitively, if an ingredient has a lower pH, like a lemon, it is considered a higher-acid food. An ingredient with a higher pH, like steak, is considered a lower-acid food. Some common high-acid foods are pomegranates, blueberries, tomatoes, and citrus.

Acid can help prevent bacterial and microbial growth in foods as well as resist enzyme changes in food that can cause discoloration. Maybe you're familiar with the trick of squeezing a lemon on a cut slice of apple to help it retain its color.

TIME AND TEMPERATURE

I previously mentioned the importance of time and temperature in canning foods safely. If you're a seasoned water bath canner but are new to pressure canning, you might be wondering what the difference is. Water bath canning is a great tool for preserving foods that are higher acid, like jams, jellies, pickled vegetables, and fruits. These higher-acid foods are capable of destroying bacterial spores. However, water bath canning simply does not provide a high enough temperature for a long enough time to safely eliminate bacterial spores in lower-acid foods, which are known for supporting bacterial growth. These spores are dangerous because they produce toxins that can cause botulism, or *Clostridium botulinum*, which can lead to serious illness and even death. The spores have no odor or taste, and they are not visible, unlike yeasts or molds. I know this can sound scary, but pressure canning is the solution! Pressure canning meets the recommended 240 degrees Fahrenheit at which you will process all recipes. Although it is important to keep a healthy respect for food safety and pressure canning, it is also important to remember that you can safely enjoy pressure canning in your home by following these simple step-by-step guidelines.

GETTING STARTED FAQ

1. **Am I doing it right? How do I know if something is wrong?**
   After the jars are cooled, you can test that the lids are vacuum sealed to the jars. Check for a vacuum seal by pressing in the center of the lid. If it releases or springs up once you lift your finger, the jar is not sealed. If the jar is not sealed, inspect the jar for cracks, nicks, or other damage, and move the product to a new jar, if necessary. You can reprocess the jars within 24 hours, place them in the refrigerator to keep, and/or eat the contents within a few days. Remember: When in doubt, throw it out. If you open a jar and suspect something is wrong, throw it out.

2. **Do processing times change based on the size of the jar I am using?**
   Yes, processing times can vary by recipe based on the jar size used. If you have questions, please refer to the recipe for specific instructions for each size jar recommended. Often, larger jars, such as quart jars, are not compatible with certain recipes. Please do not attempt to modify a recipe.

3. **Can I double or halve a recipe?**
   These recipes are written to remain true to size while also leaving room for slight variances in how many jars a recipe will fill based on the size jar you choose to can. Sometimes when you are following a recipe there will be a variance of 1 to 2 jars from what the recipe calls for and how much of a meal or ingredient you have to fill your jars. This is normal. Doubling or halving a recipe is not recommended.

4. **If I want to can a recipe with multiple ingredients, how long do I process it?**
   Always err on the side of the single ingredient that requires the longest processing time. For example, if you are pressure canning a soup with chicken, vegetables, and broth, you would want to process to the length of time it takes to safely process chicken, as it takes longer than vegetables and broth. This will ensure that everything within the jar gets safely preserved.

5. **What are some foods I should avoid pressure canning?**
Dairy, flours, nut meats, eggs, pureed foods, whole fruits, jams, cruciferous vegetables, lettuce, olives, and any thickening agents.

6. **How long will my preserved food last?**
Home–pressure canned foods will stay shelf stable for up to 1 year. I encourage you to store your jars in a cool, dark space, away from direct light or sun. Always clearly label and date your jars when canning.

7. **If my jar did not seal, can I process it again?**
There is a safe window to reprocess food for up to 24 hours after the initial canning process. Remove the bands and lids to check the jars for any damage, and if necessary, change jars. Always use a new lid. Process again following the original recipe canning instructions.

8. **Can I reuse lids and bands?**
The sealing compound on jar lids is only guaranteed to seal for one use. You should never reuse lids. Bands are okay to reuse if they are in good condition and free from rust or dents that could affect the seal.

9. **Can I pressure can pureed squash or pureed vegetables?**
Pureed foods are not recommended for home pressure canning, as heat cannot adequately penetrate the center of the jars to ensure safe preservation. It is recommended to cube squash and other vegetables in order to safely pressure can.

10. **If mold grows inside a jar, can I scrape it off and eat the contents of the jar?**
Mold is a fungus and has the potential to raise the pH of the foods it grows on. Any pressure canned foods that have mold growth should be discarded. The best rule to remember with food is when in doubt, throw it out.

Safe Canning through Science

Learning how to properly and safely pressure can foods at home is empowering. There are scientific ways pressure canning allows you to process and preserve foods so that they may be enjoyed long afterward. The science behind pressure canning is really high heat. The lower-acid foods we are aiming to preserve through pressure canning must be heated to a much higher temperature than boiling water in order to safely kill the most persistent and unsafe microorganisms. The pressurized steam heats the contents of the jars and creates an environment where microorganisms cannot exist. Initially, pressure canning can seem intimidating, but once you start to feel comfortable with the canning process, you will begin to feel more confident in knowing that the food you are creating is going to be delicious and safe for your friends and family to enjoy.

RAW PACK AND HOT PACK

Pressure canning happens in two main ways, either through a Raw/Cold Pack or through a Hot Pack method. These terms refer to what state the ingredients are in when you pack them into jars. The difference is whether a recipe requires you to put raw ingredients into a jar to process from a cold state or whether the items are cooked and hot before portioning into your jars. Some recipes may call for a blend of the two, where you place raw proteins in a jar and then top with additional hot ingredients, for example, as a soup recipe may require. Hot-packed foods call for you to heat the water inside the pressure canner to 180 degrees Fahrenheit, and raw/cold-packed foods call for the water to be heated to only 140 degrees Fahrenheit. It is important to be careful not to overheat the water during this process, which could cause the water level in your pressure canner to fall. Be sure to follow the water temperature heating instructions carefully, as placing cold jars into water that is too hot can cause the jars to break or shatter.

AVOIDING BOTULISM

Botulism is a type of poisoning that attacks the body's nerves. Symptoms of botulism poisoning include upset stomach, difficulty swallowing or breathing, blurred vision, muscle weakness, slurred speech, and sometimes death. You can't see botulism, so following the instructions is important to ensuring your food is safely preserved. The botulism toxin is caused by the microorganism *Clostridium botulinum,* and specific conditions are needed for it to grow or spread. These conditions include low oxygen (anaerobic), low-acid foods, high moisture, and temperatures in the danger zone of 40 to 120 degrees Fahrenheit. The great thing about pressure canning is that it allows you to control for all these variables, ensuring that your food is safely preserved.

To Can or Not to Can

Since pressure canning reaches such a high temperature, you can safely can lower-acid foods. Although numerous foods can be canned, there are a few exceptions. Avoid canning the following:

Dense foods: Foods like pureed vegetables and mashed potatoes prevent the heat from penetrating all the way to the center of the jar, so you cannot be sure that they will be safe to eat; therefore, they should not be pressure canned. Flour and other thickeners should be avoided for this same reason. Garlic should be avoided as well, since it loses most of its flavor when canned and can turn bitter.

Milk-based or dairy foods: These should also be avoided, as the heat can cause curdling and create a poor-quality product.

Whole berries and other delicate fruits: These do not withstand the high temperatures required in pressure canning, so the result can sometimes be disappointing. Fruits and jams are best processed using the water bath canning method.

A NOTE ON USDA CANNING GUIDELINES

I started canning in northwest Missouri, years ago, before I had ever heard of U.S. Department of Agriculture (USDA) canning guidelines. I have consumed many products made by myself and others where we followed recipes passed down by family and the community. When I finally received my Master Food Preserver certification and spent time training with others who had completed years of education, I learned that a lot of what was passed down to me from my friends were myths and not supported by scientific research. Fortunately, the USDA created a research-based Complete Guide to Home Canning, which was developed through research conducted by the National Center for Home Food Preservation in cooperation with the USDA's National Institute of Food and Agriculture. These guidelines include proven ways to safely preserve foods through pressure canning at home.

Research-based methods often take a long time to get approved, so the recipes the USDA provides can be somewhat basic and to-the-point. However, after having invested so many hours into training, certification, practice, and volunteering, I now feel comfortable supporting the hard rules that ensure the safety of canning while also exploring the ways in which my home canning practice can support my personal tastes and creativity.

As you move through your canning journey, you might encounter groups that are invested in strictly following USDA guidelines with no exceptions. You may also encounter people who have been canning outdoors on open fires and following family recipes their entire lives. Each of us has a responsibility to get curious, ask questions, and conduct our own research in order to determine our comfort level. You will find through the recipes in this book that safety and process are paramount. Flavor and creativity are also super important. This is a great book for connecting the expertise and experience of science while also embracing the creativity and magic that is home pressure canning.

Stocking Your Canning-Ready Kitchen

Stocking your pantry for pressure canning is simple. There are a handful of tools you will want to invest in that will last you many years with very little maintenance. It is a good idea to keep a small inventory of jars, lids, and rings on hand in a few sizes to meet your canning needs. Aside from these basics, select the recipe you would like to make a few days in advance, read the recipe start to finish, purchase the ingredients a day or two before, then dive right in.

INGREDIENTS

A basic rule for canning is that your final product will never be higher quality than your beginning product. This means that a wilting vegetable or browning piece of meat will never improve through the process of canning, only deteriorate. If you want a great end product, start with high-quality ingredients. Our goal is to create safe and delicious preserved foods that still have great taste and quality several months after processing. The following list includes several things to keep in mind about ingredients.

Meat, game, and seafood: These are all incredibly perishable ingredients and must be handled with care. Always start with fresh, high-quality cuts, and can within 2 to 3 days of purchasing unless you are freezing the product. As a rule, I recommend removing any skin, scales, or dark spots when canning meat, poultry, or fish.

Produce: Produce does not lie. If you purchase or harvest produce that is in poor shape, the quality will not get better through the pressure canning process. It is best to purchase or harvest your produce the day of or day before canning. Be sure to clean your produce like normal. When selecting your fruits and vegetables, look for firm produce that is bright in color, with fresh green leaves, and free from soft spots or blemishes.

Salt: Under the umbrella of pressure canning, salt is ultimately used for flavor. Salt is your best friend; it's how you bring out flavor in all foods. Since you are pressure canning, you do not need to worry about salt as a preservation tool.

Vinegar: Vinegar is important when canning, not only as an ingredient in some recipes but also as a tool to help get a good seal. Sometimes white vinegar is used for cutting any fat or oily residue from the rims of jars you are canning. We will use white vinegar in every recipe in this book for this purpose, as it is more neutral in flavor. You can use any other vinegar for this purpose if you do not have white vinegar on hand. A good rule to remember: Acid cuts fat.

Water: Pressure canning does require water to create the steam pressure, and some recipes call for the ingredients to be boiled, using the boiling liquid for the hot pack. Distilled water is ideal, but you can use tap water as well. If you have hard water, it may be a good idea to purchase distilled water.

SALT AND SUGAR

Salt and sugar are wonderful ingredients. When pressure canning, they are simply additions to a recipe to affect flavor. The quantities of salt or sugar represented in these recipes are merely to support the flavoring of food, rather than support food preservation. If you are concerned about dietary restrictions or other health considerations, you may omit the salt and sugar or adjust the levels to your preferred taste without impacting the quality or safety of the foods being canned.

I have cooked with and provided recipes for many individuals who were preparing foods with differing health concerns and who have adapted the salt or sugar levels to meet their individual needs. This is a welcomed practice. As a rule, I always encourage tasting your food throughout the preparation process so you may adjust the flavor as you proceed. Many of the recipes can be canned without salt or sugar of any kind; they can simply be added in, to taste, as you reheat or open the canned goods to enjoy for a family supper. A simple rule to remember with salt and sugar is that you cannot remove these ingredients, you can only add. It's best to add sparingly and taste often so you can adjust as needed. I prefer using a blend of Himalayan pink salt and kosher salt for all my recipes. Regular table salt contains anti-caking ingredients that can sometimes result in a slightly cloudy appearance in canned foods. If you would like to avoid the possibility of cloudiness, canning salt may be used in place of table salt.

EQUIPMENT AND TOOLS

Let's get you started with a few basic tools that you'll need for pressure canning. There are many good options available on the market at varying price points, so find something you like that fits your budget.

FIGURE 1.1

PRESSURE CANNER

A pressure canner is a large pot, typically made of aluminum, with a flat rack in the bottom and a lid (figure 1.1). It is fitted with a vent, valves, locks, and gaskets or clamps. To safely pressure can, your canner must fit at least 4 quart-size jars. Anything smaller than this capacity is not recommended, as enough heat may not be generated to properly process your jars. It is best to ensure your pressure canner is completely clean and dry before storing. I prefer to leave paper towels inside the canner to absorb any possible moisture and wrap the lid in paper or place it in a large paper bag. Always look for the (UL) Underwriters Laboratories approval on any pressure canner you purchase to ensure safety.

LARGE STOCKPOT

Most of the recipes for pressure canning will require you to cook the food before processing it. I recommend using a heavy-bottomed, high-sided, 6- to 8-quart stainless steel pot like a saucepan or stockpot. I personally use my enameled Dutch oven and cast-iron Dutch oven for most recipes, and they work great, but they are not necessary to purchase if you do not already own them.

FIGURE 1.2

GLASS JARS

You will want to stock up on glass Mason jars if you are planning on canning (figure 1.2). I use Ball brand jars in my kitchen because they are consistent, affordable, and readily available in my area, although there are other brands, like Kerr, which are also okay to use and reuse. I find it is easiest to buy one brand and stick with it. I keep an assortment of wide-mouth half-pint, pint, and quart jars ready to use, as they are the most common sizes used in canning. My personal preference is for wide-mouth jars, as I find them easier to clean and fill, and I like the way they look. You should never reuse commercial jars for canning, as the glass is much thinner, making it susceptible to breaking, and you will not get a reliable seal.

FIGURE 1.3

LIDS AND RINGS

Lids and rings (figure 1.3) will need to be replaced. Single-use lids are most common in canning, are sold separately from jars and rings, and must be replaced every time. Never reuse a single-use lid that has already been processed, as it will not seal correctly. Rings are also sold separately from jars and need to be replaced any time they are damaged or nicked or show signs of rust. There are a few producers that make reusable lids and gaskets that last for 6 to 8 uses, but these reusable parts are a hotly debated topic and require slightly different processes once the jars are canned.

TERRY CLOTH WASHCLOTH AND TEA TOWELS

Once your jars have finished processing, they will need a soft place to land. You will want to prepare a space where you can spread out a tea towel to rest your jars on. The tea towel can also be used for dipping in white vinegar and cleaning the rims of the jars before placing the lids on. The vinegar cuts through any fat or oily residue on the rims that could prevent your jars from sealing properly. A tea towel or disposable paper towel is recommended for cleaning the rims of jars, as it will not leave behind any fibers that could impact the seal.

CANNING KIT

You can typically find canning kits bundled together online and at your local market or hardware store. This kit will need to include a funnel (figure 1.4), a bubble popper/measurer (figure 1.5), a magnetic lid lifter (figure 1.6), and jar-lifter tongs (figure 1.7). The funnel is necessary for getting food into the jars. The bubble popper/measurer is a 2-in-1 tool that helps you release any air bubbles along the inside of your jars, and the opposite side has a stepped edge that helps you accurately measure headspace. The magnetic lid lifter helps you pick up and place your lids on top of your jars so you avoid getting oils or residue from your hands onto the lid or jar rims that could affect your seal. The tongs are perfectly shaped for grabbing the jars and lifting them in and out of your pressure canner without tilting them, as that could also affect your seal if the food gets under the lid onto the rims of the jars.

FIGURE 1.4–1.8

Additional items that may be nice to have include oven mitts (figure 1.8), a kitchen scale, a digital timer, and a ladle. Oven mitts are handy to have, as you will be handling hot surfaces. A kitchen scale is useful for measuring and weighing ingredients for your recipes. A digital timer will help accurately measure and track your processing times. A ladle is useful for loading jars with your funnel.

GETTING AHEAD OF HEADSPACE

Headspace is an important part of canning. It is the empty space left inside at the top of your jar and in pressure canning will almost always be 1 inch from the top, though a few recipes will call for 1¼ inch of headspace. Always follow each recipe exactly and leave the proper amount of recommended headspace. You will use the measurer to ensure proper space is left in each jar; be sure not to skip this step. This space allows the food to expand while it is heated without being forced out of the jar, where it would potentially disturb or impact the seal.

Pressure Canner 101

Pressure canning got its start a long time ago thanks to a French physicist and mathematician named Denis Papin. He created a large, cast-iron kettle with a lid that locked onto the kettle. The ability of these kettles to cook food quickly and break down tough bones was a huge advancement. These first pressure cookers were hard to control and often caused explosions due to the pressure buildup, which is responsible for some of the fear surrounding pressure cooking. Fast-forward a few years and the need for preserved food arose when traveling soldiers required food that they could carry with them that would stay fresh on their journey. The early version of canned food in glass jars involved wax coating to seal and wires to reinforce their closure. Fast-forward again to the 19th century, when John Mason created a jar with a rubber seal and a metal top that threaded on to secure the jar. That's why we often refer to them as Mason jars. Rest assured, the technology and safety aspects of pressure canning equipment have come a long way, and once you get the hang of the process, you will be rewarded with all the benefits!

WEIGHTED GAUGE (A.K.A. JIGGLER) VS. DIAL GAUGE

There are a few options when it comes to the model of pressure canner. Some may have a weighted gauge, whereas others may have a dial gauge. These gauges are responsible for indicating and regulating the pressure in your canner. Weighted gauges fit over the vent on your canner, permitting the pressure to rise to the desired set point. The weight on the gauge can be adjusted, and these gauges are designed to rock or jiggle when they release pressure to maintain the desired level. Dial gauge canners use a dial to indicate the pressure inside your canner and a pressure regulator that sits over the vent to allow the pressure to build. There is a safety fuse, or plug, on dial gauge canners that allows the pressure to release. This safety feature serves an important role in that it keeps the canner from becoming overpressured and can either melt or be blown out to release pressure. Weighted gauge canners are the most affordable option between the two, as they involve less technology, but if used properly they will always be accurate. All canners need yearly testing and maintenance to ensure they are working properly.

GASKET VS. NO GASKET

Canners have different designs, and one thing that sets them apart is how their lids close and secure onto the canner. Many canners have rubber gaskets that help create a seal. Other canner models use fully metal lids that are secured by large clamps that hold the lid securely onto the canner. A benefit of purchasing a canner that uses clamps is that clamps, unlike gaskets, do not need to be replaced regularly.

GET TO KNOW THE PSI

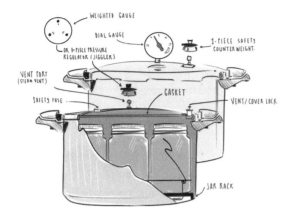

PSI stands for pound-force per square inch. Every pressure canning recipe will require specific pounds of pressure. While pressure canning, this indicates the pounds of pressure inside your canner. This number will vary based on the type of canner you use, either weighted or dial gauge. Dial gauge pressure canners have the ability to adjust down to a smaller 1-pound PSI, giving them greater flexibility when adjusting for altitude than their weighted gauge counterparts.

A GO-TO PRESSURE CANNER

Investing in a good pressure canner does not have to break the bank. There are lots of models to choose from, and it can be fun to compare the different options available to you based on your budget. When I first started pressure canning, I got to experiment with various pressure canners, which helped me choose the right style for me. I first purchased the Presto 16-quart weighted gauge pressure canner at my local store for $75. This was a good pressure canner, and I processed hundreds of jars with it over the years. When I made the choice to upgrade, I decided to purchase the Presto 23-quart dial gauge pressure canner and the Presto 12-quart electric pressure canner. These are the two pressure canners I currently use and highly recommend. I was skeptical about the electric pressure canner in the beginning, but after doing some research, it became clear that it matched the USDA guidelines for pressure canning, and it is a game changer! I would like to clarify that this is a pressure canner, not a *pressure cooker*. There is a big difference, and it is never safe to can in a pressure cooker even though the manual might suggest that the equipment can do so. Please do not attempt to use a pressure cooker for canning under any circumstance.

5 Rules for Successful Pressure Canning

There are a handful of key things you should be aware of in starting your canning journey. The recipe details are important to success, as is the equipment you use, proper headspace, rim cleanliness, and confirming you're working with sealed jars. Missing any of these details may cause you challenges, so be prepared and read the detailed information on these topics.

1. Read the recipe thoroughly

Just as you would in any recipe, the most important step is to read the full recipe from start to finish. I recommend reading a pressure canning recipe days before you plan to make it. This will help you identify any special ingredients needed, how much active or inactive time to prepare, and how the recipe is intended to flow. It might sound like a basic step you can skip, but it is the most important step of all. Once you start a pressure canning recipe, you are committed to staying with the canner throughout the duration of the process. The last thing you want is to get halfway through a recipe only to realize you are missing an important ingredient or tool and that you will have to start over later because you did not read the recipe all the way through. A good practice is to keep a notebook with you to jot down ideas or notes about the process.

2. Check your equipment

Days before you plan to work through a pressure canning recipe, inventory your equipment to make sure that you have the right number and size of jars, that you have adequate lids and rings, and that your equipment is all in good shape. Set a calendar reminder for each year to have your equipment inspected for repairs or replacement parts. Libraries, counties, and local groups typically offer this service, free of charge or for a minimal donation, once a year. When pressure canning, make sure your jars, lids, and bands are clean. There is no reason to sterilize your jars since they will be heat-processed in the pressure canner at 240 degrees Fahrenheit.

3. Get the headspace right

Headspace is the empty space between the top of your food and the top of your jar. This space is important because it allows the food room to expand as it heats without forcing it out of the jar and under the lid, potentially compromising the seal. The bubble popper/measurer tool can be used to pop or release any trapped air bubbles along the inside of your jars. Once you pop these bubbles, the content level may drop, leaving you with too much headspace. If this happens, you will want to add more food or liquid to bring it back to the correct headspace. The measurer will help you identify if you have left proper headspace by measuring from the top of your food to the top of your jar. For more information on headspace, see page 13.

4. Clean the rims thoroughly

Jar rims must be cleaned before fitting with lids. When you are filling jars, it is common for food to spill or splash onto the rims of your jars. If you were to process the jar with food on the rim, it is unlikely you would have a successful seal. Use a towel dampened with vinegar to wipe down the jar rims, cutting through any oily residue and leaving the rims clean so they can form a proper seal with the lid.

5. Make sure your jars have sealed

After 12 to 24 hours, press down on the lid of each jar. If the lid stays down, your seal was successful. If the lid pops up, put the jar in the fridge, and eat the contents within a week; or check the jar for any damage and replace, if necessary, then reprocess the jar within the 24-hour window. After the cooling process is completed, you may remove the bands from the jars. The rings are not meant to stay on the jars. Once the seal has been made, the rings have served their purpose. Remember that the pop or ping sound that often comes from canned jars is not necessary for a good seal. Sometimes they seal just fine without popping.

ADJUSTING FOR ALTITUDE

Recipes are written and developed based on sea-level altitude. At sea level, air pressure is at its highest depth. As you gain altitude, air pressure decreases. Therefore, canning at any higher altitude will require adjustments to your PSI, or pound-force per square inch. Every 1,000 feet of gained elevation may require an adjustment. An altitude chart has been provided for your reference on page 136.

Pressure Canner Step by Step

The following are step-by-step pressure canning instructions for you to reference for every recipe in this book.

1. Place your canner over the burner. Once you have prepared your jars for canning, per the recipe instructions, put the rack in the bottom of the canner and fill the canner with 2 to 3 inches of water.

2. Prepare the recipe or ingredients and fill the jars with the food.

3. Using the bubble popper/measurer tool, pop any air bubbles inside the jars and adjust the fill, if needed, to reach the proper headspace. Use the measurer to measure headspace accordingly.

4. Dampen a corner of a tea towel or paper towel with white vinegar and use this to clean the jar rims before placing the lids on top.

5. Place lids onto jars and, using a tea towel, lightly finger-tighten the bands onto the lids. Do not tighten past finger tight.

6. Using the jar-lifter tongs, carefully lift the jars onto the rack in the canner without tilting the jars. The tongs should fit just below the neck of the jar. The jars should always be kept upright.

7. Once your jars are loaded into the canner, secure the lid onto the canner. The weight should not be on the vent at this time.

8. Turn the heat to the highest setting, and heat the water to 140 degrees for Raw/Cold Pack recipes and 180 degrees for Hot Pack recipes. Once the water is boiling, it will cause steam to flow out of the vent. This is called venting, or exhausting, your canner. Let the canner exhaust for 10 continuous minutes.

9. Once the 10 minutes of exhausting has passed, place the pressure regulator or weighted gauge on the vent. This will cause the canner to pressurize within the next 10 minutes.

10. When the dial indicates the appropriate pressure has been reached on a dial gauge canner, or the weighted gauge starts jiggling or rocking the appropriate number of times per minute, you can start your timer to track the processing time. During this processing time, you want to keep the pressure at or above the recommended PSI.

11. Once the processing time has been completed, turn off the heat, and remove the canner from the heat, if necessary, so it can begin cooling. This process is called depressurizing.

12. Never attempt to force cool your canner. This process is important to the proper sealing and processing of your food. Do not rush this process.

13. After the depressurization has been completed, carefully tilt the weight to make sure there is no more steam to escape before removing it completely.

14. Wait for 10 minutes, then carefully remove the lid.

15. Using the jar-lifter tongs, and without tilting the jars, carefully remove the jars. Place them 1 inch apart on a clean towel, out of direct light, and leave undisturbed for at least 12 to 24 hours. Then, check the jars for seals and remove rings.

16. Label the lids. Store foods in a cool, dark place for up to 1 year until ready to serve.

17. If any jars did not seal properly, place them in the refrigerator. You can reprocess the jars within 24 hours following the process from start to finish again with the full processing time.

18. Clean your equipment, wrap in paper, and store away until your next canning session.

About the Recipes

This book is a step-by-step beginner's guide to the world of pressure canning. The recipes presented here are intended to be flavorful and classic and provide you with go-to meals your family and friends will love to eat on a regular basis. If you have never tried pressure canning before or are new to pressure canning and seeking a little more guidance, this is the book for you. Each recipe is designed to include 10 or fewer ingredients to keep things simple and delicious.

Many recipes offer ingredient substitutions, safety reminders, healthy suggestions, and other tips to help you feel confident storing and enjoying your canned goods.

If you are brand new to pressure canning, a great place to start is with the recipes for Zesty Black Beans (page 50) or All-Purpose Canned Chicken (page 92). These are simple recipes with minimal ingredients that will have you pressure canning in no time. They also pair well for a quick and healthy salad over a bed of greens or atop a bowl of rice with avocado for a power lunch. The possibilities are endless, and thanks to pressure canning, you will have an abundance of high-quality meals and ingredients ready at your fingertips.

CHAPTER 2

Vegetables

Roasted Bell Peppers

YIELD: 10 (1-pint) jars | **PREP:** Active time, 45 minutes / Inactive time, 1 hour

Roasted bell peppers are incredibly versatile and amplify any dish. Try using them in a power lunch bowl or salad, stuffing them for a quick weeknight meal, or serving them as part of a charcuterie board or an appetizer when hosting friends.

9 pounds bell peppers, any color, rinsed with cool water and patted dry

1. Heat the stove or grill to medium-high heat. An oven on high broil can also be used.

2. Char the outside of the peppers evenly until blistered, for 2 to 5 minutes per side, depending on the flame and the desired darkness of the peppers. If using the oven, broil for about 20 minutes.

3. Once the peppers have been charred black and crispy, place them in a bowl or on a baking sheet and cover with plastic wrap, a bowl, or a damp towel for 15 minutes to steam. The steaming process helps loosen the skin to remove. The peppers should be soft to the touch. If needed, continue to roast a bit longer until softened.

4. After the peppers have steamed, gently remove most of the blistered pepper skin by peeling it off, leaving a few charred spots. This will help flavor the peppers in the jar.

5. Take a paring knife and cut around the stem, removing the stem, the core, and the seeds.

6. Bring a kettle of water to a boil. Remove from the heat.

7. Pack the hot jars with peppers; 3 to 4 whole peppers will fit into one pint jar. The peppers

can be diced, sliced, or chopped. This will allow for a significantly greater number of peppers to fit into each jar and will yield far fewer total jars.

8. Pour boiling water over the top of the peppers, leaving 1 inch of headspace.

9. Using the measurer, pop any air bubbles inside the jars and adjust the fill, if needed, to reach the proper headspace.

10. Dampen a corner of a paper towel with white vinegar and clean the jar rims. Place lids onto jars and, using a tea towel, lightly finger-tighten the bands onto the lids. Do not tighten past finger tight. Wipe jar rims to remove any oily residue.

11. Carefully lift the jars onto the rack in the canner without tilting the jars. Secure the lid onto the canner and heat the water to 180 degrees for Hot Pack recipes. Let the canner exhaust for 10 continuous minutes.

12. Place the pressure regulator or weighted gauge on the vent and process for 35 minutes for pint jars in a dial gauge pressure canner at 11 pounds PSI or in a weighted gauge pressure canner at 10 pounds PSI.

13. Once completed, remove the canner from the heat. Carefully tilt the weight to make sure there is no more steam to escape before removing completely. Wait for 10 minutes, then carefully remove the lid.

14. Place the jars 1 inch apart on a clean towel, out of direct light, and leave undisturbed for at least 12 to 24 hours.

SAFETY FIRST: Wash hands often, and consider wearing gloves when working with peppers, especially if using hot peppers. Capsaicin, the compound that gives peppers their heat, can build up on skin and become painful.

Charred Whole Green Chiles

YIELD: 10 (1-pint) jars | **PREP:** Active time, 35 minutes / Inactive time, 1 hour

Peppers are a lower-acid food that respond well to pressure canning as a preservation method. These green chiles are excellent when added to enchiladas, burritos, or cheesy dip. The chiles can be diced or left whole. Use Hatch, Poblano, or Anaheim chile peppers for the best flavor.

9 pounds green chile peppers, rinsed with cool water and patted dry

1. Heat the stove or grill to medium-high heat. An oven on high broil can also be used.

2. Char the outside of the peppers evenly until blistered, for 2 to 5 minutes per side, depending on the flame and the desired darkness of the peppers. If using the oven, broil for about 20 minutes.

3. Once the peppers have been charred black and crispy, place them in a bowl or on a baking sheet and cover with plastic wrap, a bowl, or a damp towel for 15 minutes to steam. The steaming process helps loosen the skin to remove. The peppers should be soft to the touch. If needed, continue to roast a bit longer until softened.

4. After the peppers have steamed, gently remove most of the blistered pepper skin by peeling it off, leaving a few charred spots. This will help flavor the peppers in the jar. Leave the chiles whole with the stem attached, or dice, if desired.

5. Bring a kettle of water to a boil. Remove from the heat.

6. Gently fold the chiles and insert them into hot jars until loosely packed. Cover the chiles with boiling water, leaving 1 inch of headspace. Using the measurer, pop any air bubbles inside the jars and adjust the fill, if needed, to reach the proper headspace.

7. Dampen a corner of a paper towel with white vinegar and clean the jar rims. Place lids onto jars and, using a tea towel, lightly finger-tighten the bands onto the lids. Do not tighten past finger tight. Wipe jar rims to remove any oily residue.

8. Carefully lift the jars onto the rack in the canner without tilting the jars. Secure the lid onto the canner and heat the water to 180 degrees for Hot Pack recipes. Let the canner exhaust for 10 continuous minutes.

9. Place the pressure regulator or weighted gauge on the vent and process for 35 minutes for pint jars in a dial gauge pressure canner at 11 pounds PSI or in a weighted gauge pressure canner at 10 pounds PSI.

10. Once completed, remove the canner from the heat. Carefully tilt the weight to make sure there is no more steam to escape before removing completely. Wait for 10 minutes, then carefully remove the lid.

11. Place the jars 1 inch apart on a clean towel, out of direct light, and leave undisturbed for at least 12 to 24 hours.

Southern Corn Relish

YIELD: 10 (1-pint) jars | **PREP:** Active time, 25 minutes / Inactive time, 1 hour 15 minutes

Corn relish is incredibly versatile. Use it to liven up a burger or salad, try it with corn chips as a salsa, or serve it with eggs for breakfast. Be creative and add it to a variety of foods.

10 ears fresh corn on the cob, about 8 cups, kernels removed

2 jalapeño peppers or hot peppers, diced

1 yellow onion, diced

1 red bell pepper, diced

1 green bell pepper, diced

1 tablespoon mustard seeds

4 cups white or apple cider vinegar

2 cups brown sugar

2 teaspoons salt

1. Place a large stockpot on the stove, half fill with water, and add the corn, jalapeño peppers, onion, red bell pepper, green bell pepper, mustard seeds, vinegar, brown sugar, and salt. Turn on the heat and bring to a boil, stirring occasionally. Reduce the heat to medium and continue stirring until the sugar is dissolved and the vegetables are tender, for about 15 minutes. Remove from the heat.

2. Ladle the relish into hot jars, leaving 1 inch of headspace.

3. Using the measurer, pop any air bubbles inside the jars and adjust the fill, if needed, to reach the proper headspace.

4. Dampen a corner of a paper towel with white vinegar and clean the jar rims. Place lids onto jars and, using a tea towel, lightly finger-tighten the bands onto the lids. Do not tighten past finger tight. Wipe jar rims to remove any oily residue.

5. Carefully lift the jars onto the rack in the canner without tilting the jars. Secure the lid onto the canner and heat the water to 180 degrees for Hot Pack recipes. Let the canner exhaust for 10 continuous minutes.

6. Place the pressure regulator or weighted gauge on the vent and process for 55 minutes for pint jars in a dial gauge pressure canner at 11 pounds PSI or in a weighted gauge pressure canner at 10 pounds PSI.

7. Once completed, remove the canner from the heat. Carefully tilt the weight to make sure there is no more steam to escape before removing completely. Wait for 10 minutes, then carefully remove the lid.

8. Place the jars 1 inch apart on a clean towel, out of direct light, and leave undisturbed for at least 12 to 24 hours.

LOW-SODIUM AND SUGAR TIP: Skip the sugar and salt in the ingredients, and instead add at the time of serving, if desired.

HOT PACK

Sweet Creamed Corn

YIELD: 10 (1-pint) jars | **PREP:** Active time, 20 minutes / Inactive time, 1 hour 15 minutes

When it comes time to serve this creamed-style corn, serve it as is, or heat it on the stove with butter and cream cheese or coconut milk to give it that extra creaminess.

9 pounds frozen corn kernels

1 tablespoon nutmeg

1 teaspoon cayenne pepper (optional)

1 tablespoon garlic powder

1 tablespoon onion powder

3 tablespoons sugar

2 tablespoons salt

1. Put the corn, nutmeg, cayenne (if using), garlic powder, onion powder, sugar, and salt in a large stockpot on the stove. Add water to the top of the ingredients and bring to a boil. Reduce the heat to a low simmer.

2. Using an immersion blender, puree about half of the kernels to give them a creamy texture. If an immersion blender isn't available, remove portions of the corn and puree in a blender, then return to the stockpot, repeating until the desired creaminess is reached. Once finished, remove the stockpot from the heat.

3. Ladle the corn into hot jars, leaving 1 inch of headspace. Using the measurer, pop any air bubbles inside the jars and adjust the fill, if needed, to reach the proper headspace.

4. Dampen a corner of a paper towel with white vinegar and clean the jar rims. Place lids onto jars and, using a tea towel, lightly finger-tighten the bands onto the lids. Do not tighten past finger tight. Wipe jar rims to remove any oily residue.

5. Carefully lift the jars onto the rack in the canner without tilting the jars. Secure the lid onto the canner and heat the water to 180 degrees for Hot Pack recipes. Let the canner exhaust for 10 continuous minutes.

6. Place the pressure regulator or weighted gauge on the vent and process for 55 minutes for pint jars in a dial gauge pressure canner at 11 pounds PSI or in a weighted gauge pressure canner at 10 pounds PSI.

7. Once completed, remove the canner from the heat. Carefully tilt the weight to make sure there is no more steam to escape before removing completely. Wait for 10 minutes, then carefully remove the lid.

8. Place the jars 1 inch apart on a clean towel, out of direct light, and leave undisturbed for at least 12 to 24 hours.

VARIATION TIP: To make a delicious dip, try adding Charred Whole Green Chiles (see page 26), topping the dish with some shredded cheese and breadcrumbs, then placing under the broiler until the cheese is melted.

Bacon and Onion Green Beans

YIELD: 10 (1-pint) jars | **PREP:** Active time, 40 minutes / Inactive time, 40 minutes

Green beans are the epitome of comfort food. They can be prepared in a variety of ways, including fresh, canned, or pickled. Besides being delicious, green beans are legumes that are high in fiber and many different vitamins that support overall health.

1 pound bacon, diced
2 yellow onions, diced
9 pounds fresh green beans, trimmed and cut into 1- to 2-inch pieces
¼ cup salt
1 tablespoon garlic salt (optional)
1 tablespoon freshly ground black pepper

1. Heat a large stockpot over medium-high heat. Once hot, put the bacon in the pot and cook until firm and fragrant but not browned. Add the onions and continue to cook until both are starting to brown. Do not drain the rendered fat, as this gives the finished recipe great flavor.

2. Add the green beans, salt, garlic salt (if using), and pepper to the bacon and onion mixture and cover with water, then a lid. Bring to a boil, then reduce the heat. Simmer for 10 minutes, then remove from the heat.

3. Ladle the green beans into hot jars, leaving 1 inch of headspace. Using the measurer, pop any air bubbles inside the jars and adjust the fill, if needed, to reach the proper headspace.

4. Dampen a corner of a paper towel with white vinegar and clean the jar rims. Place lids onto jars and, using a tea towel, lightly finger-tighten the bands onto the lids. Do not tighten past finger tight. Wipe jar rims to remove any oily residue.

5. Carefully lift the jars onto the rack in the canner without tilting the jars. Secure the lid onto the canner and heat the water to 180 degrees for Hot Pack recipes. Let the canner exhaust for 10 continuous minutes.

6. Place the pressure regulator or weighted gauge on the vent and process for 20 minutes for pint jars in a dial gauge pressure canner at 11 pounds PSI or in a weighted gauge pressure canner at 10 pounds PSI.

7. Once completed, remove the canner from the heat.

8. Carefully tilt the weight to make sure there is no more steam to escape before removing completely.

9. Wait for 10 minutes, then carefully remove the lid.

10. Place the jars 1 inch apart on a clean towel, out of direct light, and leave undisturbed for at least 12 to 24 hours.

> **LOW-SODIUM TIP:** A lighter-sodium version can be achieved by reducing or eliminating the salt.

HOT PACK

Stewed Tomatoes with Basil

YIELD: 12 (1-pint) jars | **PREP:** Active time, 1 hour / Inactive time, 40 minutes

As always, the higher the quality of the ingredient used in a recipe, the better the final product. Select beautiful, ripe tomatoes for this recipe, if possible. Try to make this recipe during the warm summer months when tomatoes are abundant, and preserve them for the cooler months. The best tomatoes for this recipe are big, meaty, heirloom tomatoes, but beefsteak or roma also work well. The sugar in this recipe helps cut the tomatoes' acidity, so don't skip it, as omitting it will affect the flavor. When serving these tomatoes, heat on the stove with a bit of butter for a rich, satisfying addition and finish with a fresh basil garnish.

8 pounds fresh, ripe tomatoes

1 bunch fresh basil, about 12 leaves, chopped

1 cup sugar

2 teaspoons salt

1 teaspoon freshly ground black pepper (optional)

1. Rinse the tomatoes. Then, using a small knife, cut an X score pattern into the bottom of each tomato and cut out the stem at the top of the tomato. This will help the skins peel more easily after blanching.

2. Fill a large stockpot two-thirds full of water and bring to a boil. Fill a large bowl with ice water and set next to the stove for cooling the blanched tomatoes.

3. Gently add up to 12 tomatoes at a time to the boiling water. Blanch the tomatoes for 1 minute, then remove using a slotted spoon and set in the bowl of ice water.

4. Once the tomatoes have cooled slightly, the skins should start to loosen at the score mark and should be easy to peel off and discard.

5. Repeat until all tomatoes are blanched and skins have been removed. Empty the water from the blanching pot and return the pot to the stove.

6. Roughly chop the tomatoes and return to the stockpot. Heat to medium-high and add the basil, sugar, salt, and pepper (if using), then reduce the heat to a medium simmer and let cook for 30 minutes, or until the tomatoes are softened. Remove from the heat.

7. Ladle the tomatoes into hot jars, leaving 1 inch of headspace. Using the measurer, pop any air bubbles inside the jars and adjust the fill, if needed, to reach the proper headspace.

8. Dampen a corner of a paper towel with white vinegar and clean the jar rims. Place lids onto jars and, using a tea towel, lightly finger-tighten the bands onto the lids. Do not tighten past finger tight. Wipe jar rims to remove any oily residue.

9. Carefully lift the jars onto the rack in the canner without tilting the jars. Secure the lid onto the canner and heat the water to 180 degrees for Hot Pack recipes. Let the canner exhaust for 10 continuous minutes.

10. Place the pressure regulator or weighted gauge on the vent and process for 20 minutes for pint jars in a dial gauge pressure canner at 11 pounds PSI or in a weighted gauge pressure canner at 10 pounds PSI.

11. Once completed, remove the canner from the heat. Carefully tilt the weight to make sure there is no more steam to escape before removing completely. Wait for 10 minutes, then carefully remove the lid.

12. Place the jars 1 inch apart on a clean towel, out of direct light, and leave undisturbed for at least 12 to 24 hours.

Spiced Glazed Carrots

YIELD: 10 (1-pint) jars | **PREP:** Active time, 20 minutes / Inactive time, 45 minutes

Maple syrup works best with this recipe to keep it vegan friendly but honey works well, too. If using maple syrup, be sure to use a high-quality, real maple syrup. If less heat is preferred, reduce the amount of crushed pepper, or replace it with an herb like rosemary or oregano.

11 pounds baby or young carrots, cut into 1-inch pieces
1 cup maple syrup
1 tablespoon crushed Aleppo pepper or red pepper flakes
2 teaspoons salt

1. Put the carrots in a large stockpot over high heat. Add water to cover the carrots and bring to a boil. Once boiling, reduce the heat and simmer for 5 minutes.

2. Remove from the heat and drain the carrots, reserving the water to cover the carrots before canning. Add the maple syrup, pepper, and salt, then heat over medium-high heat for 5 minutes, or until the carrots start to caramelize. If they start to stick, use the reserved liquid by adding a tablespoon at a time until deglazed. Once the carrots are caramelized, remove from the heat.

3. Pack the carrots into hot jars and cover with the reserved boiling liquid, leaving 1 inch of headspace. Using the measurer, pop any air bubbles inside the jars and adjust the fill, if needed, to reach the proper headspace.

4. Dampen a corner of a paper towel with white vinegar and clean the jar rims. Place lids onto jars and, using a tea towel, lightly finger-tighten the bands onto the lids. Do not tighten past finger tight. Wipe jar rims to remove any oily residue.

5. Carefully lift the jars onto the rack in the canner without tilting the jars. Secure the lid onto the canner and heat the water to 180 degrees for Hot Pack recipes. Let the canner exhaust for 10 continuous minutes.

6. Place the pressure regulator or weighted gauge on the vent and process for 25 minutes for pint jars in a dial gauge pressure canner at 11 pounds PSI or in a weighted gauge pressure canner at 10 pounds PSI.

7. Once completed, turn off the heat and remove the canner from the heat. Carefully tilt the weight to make sure there is no more steam to escape before removing completely. Wait for 10 minutes, then carefully remove the lid.

8. Place the jars 1 inch apart on a clean towel, out of direct light, and leave undisturbed for at least 12 to 24 hours.

Mirepoix

YIELD: 16 (1-pint) jars | **PREP:** Active time, 15 minutes / Inactive time, 1 hour
35 minutes

Mirepoix is a classic ingredient to have on hand and is an asset in any
well-stocked pantry. Adding homemade mirepoix immediately elevates any
homemade soup, stew, or potpie and is a great way to use up bits and pieces left
over from other recipes.

**1 tablespoon butter or
ghee**

**8 cups finely chopped
carrots**

**8 cups finely chopped
celery**

**4 large onions, finely
chopped**

2 teaspoons salt

1. Heat a large stockpot over medium-high heat.
   Once hot, toss in the butter or ghee. Once
   it starts bubbling, add the carrots, celery,
   onions, and salt and continue cooking for
   about 5 minutes, or until the vegetables are
   translucent.

2. Add water to just barely cover ingredients and
   bring to a boil over high heat. Once boiling,
   remove from the heat.

3. Ladle the mirepoix into hot jars, leaving 1 inch
   of headspace. Using the measurer, pop any
   air bubbles inside the jars and adjust the fill, if
   needed, to reach the proper headspace.

4. Dampen a corner of a paper towel with white
   vinegar and clean the jar rims. Place lids onto
   jars and, using a tea towel, lightly finger-tighten
   the bands onto the lids. Do not tighten past
   finger tight. Wipe jar rims to remove any oily
   residue.

5. Carefully lift the jars onto the rack in the canner without tilting the jars. Secure the lid onto the canner and heat the water to 180 degrees for Hot Pack recipes. Let the canner exhaust for 10 continuous minutes.

6. Place the pressure regulator or weighted gauge on the vent and process for 1 hour 15 minutes for pint jars in a dial gauge pressure canner at 11 pounds PSI or in a weighted gauge pressure canner at 10 pounds PSI.

7. Once completed, remove the canner from the heat. Carefully tilt the weight to make sure there is no more steam to escape before removing completely. Wait for 10 minutes, then carefully remove the lid.

8. Place the jars 1 inch apart on a clean towel, out of direct light, and leave undisturbed for at least 12 to 24 hours.

Savory Mushrooms

YIELD: 10 (1-pint) jars | **PREP:** Active time, 15 minutes / Inactive time, 1 hour 5 minutes

These easy-to-prepare mushrooms are perfect to add to stir-fries or stews or to dress up with fresh herbs to serve as a side dish with a favorite weeknight meal. The Worcestershire sauce adds a savory, tangy, umami flavor that makes these mushrooms special.

8 pounds firm Baby Bella mushrooms, stemmed and rinsed
1 tablespoon salt
1 cup Worcestershire sauce
Ascorbic acid (optional)

1. In a large stockpot, combine the mushrooms, salt, and Worcestershire sauce. Add a pinch of ascorbic acid (if using). Cover with water, bring to a boil, and cook for 5 minutes. Remove from the heat.

2. Ladle the mushrooms into hot jars, leaving 1 inch of headspace. Using the measurer, pop any air bubbles inside the jars and adjust the fill, if needed, to reach the proper headspace.

3. Dampen a corner of a paper towel with white vinegar and clean the jar rims. Place lids onto jars and, using a tea towel, lightly finger-tighten the bands onto the lids. Do not tighten past finger tight. Wipe jar rims to remove any oily residue.

4. Carefully lift the jars onto the rack in the canner without tilting the jars. Secure the lid onto the canner and heat the water to 180 degrees for Hot Pack recipes. Let the canner exhaust for 10 continuous minutes.

5. Place the pressure regulator or weighted gauge on the vent and process for 45 minutes for pint jars in a dial gauge pressure canner at 11 pounds PSI or in a weighted gauge pressure canner at 10 pounds PSI.

6. Once completed, remove the canner from the heat. Carefully tilt the weight to make sure there is no more steam to escape before removing completely. Wait for 10 minutes, then carefully remove the lid.

7. Place the jars 1 inch apart on a clean towel, out of direct light, and leave undisturbed for at least 12 to 24 hours.

HOT
PACK

Whole Yukon Gold Potatoes

YIELD: 7 (1-quart) jars | **PREP:** Active time, 20 minutes / Inactive time, 1 hour

Potatoes are such a handy vegetable to have prepared in advance. Try panfrying these potatoes with onions and serve alongside pinto beans and corn bread. Alternatively, let them shine as the main ingredient in a potato salad.

20 pounds small Yukon Gold potatoes, 1 to 2 inches in diameter

7 teaspoons salt, 1 teaspoon per jar

1. Put the potatoes in a large stockpot and cover with water. Bring to a boil and cook for 10 minutes. Remove from the heat.

2. Heat a separate pot of water to boil to use for covering the potatoes in jars.

3. Pack the potatoes into hot jars, add 1 teaspoon of salt to each jar, then cover with boiling water, leaving 1 inch of headspace. Using the measurer, pop any air bubbles inside the jars and adjust the fill, if needed, to reach the proper headspace.

4. Dampen a corner of a paper towel with white vinegar and clean the jar rims. Place lids onto jars and, using a tea towel, lightly finger-tighten the bands onto the lids. Do not tighten past finger tight. Wipe jar rims to remove any oily residue.

5. Carefully lift the jars onto the rack in the canner without tilting the jars. Secure the lid onto the canner and heat the water to 180 degrees for Hot Pack recipes. Let the canner exhaust for 10 continuous minutes.

6. Place the pressure regulator or weighted gauge on the vent and process for 40 minutes for quart jars in a dial gauge pressure canner at 11 pounds PSI or in a weighted gauge pressure canner at 10 pounds PSI.

7. Once completed, remove the canner from the heat. Carefully tilt the weight to make sure there is no more steam to escape before removing completely. Wait for 10 minutes, then carefully remove the lid.

8. Place the jars 1 inch apart on a clean towel, out of direct light, and leave undisturbed for at least 12 to 24 hours.

CHAPTER 3

Beans and Staples

HOT PACK

Cinnamon and Sugar Sweet Potatoes

YIELD: 10 (1-pint) jars | **PREP:** Active time, 30 minutes / Inactive time, 40 minutes

These sweet potatoes are reminiscent of holidays and celebrations with friends and family. However, they are great any time of year alongside a lean cut of meat with a fresh green salad. These sweet potatoes provide that perfect toothsome bite with a sweetness that will leave everyone feeling satisfied.

11 pounds small to medium sweet potatoes

3 tablespoons brown sugar

1 tablespoon cinnamon

1 tablespoon nutmeg

1 tablespoon salt

1. Fill a large stockpot with water. Add whole sweet potatoes with the skin on, bring to a boil, and cook for 15 to 20 minutes.

2. Remove from the heat and let the sweet potatoes cool slightly. Remove their skins and discard. Cut the sweet potatoes into 1-inch cubes.

3. Heat a large pot of water and add the brown sugar, cinnamon, nutmeg, and salt. Bring to a boil and stir until the sugar has dissolved.

4. Pack the cubed sweet potatoes into hot jars. Cover with boiling sugar water, leaving 1 inch of headspace. Using the measurer, pop any air bubbles inside the jars and adjust the fill, if needed, to reach the proper headspace.

5. Dampen a corner of a paper towel with white vinegar and clean the jar rims. Place lids onto jars and, using a tea towel, lightly finger-tighten

the bands onto the lids. Do not tighten past finger tight. Wipe jar rims to remove any oily residue.

6. Carefully lift the jars onto the rack in the canner without tilting the jars. Secure the lid onto the canner and heat the water to 180 degrees for Hot Pack recipes. Let the canner exhaust for 10 continuous minutes.

7. Place the pressure regulator or weighted gauge on the vent and process for 20 minutes for pint jars in a dial gauge pressure canner at 11 pounds PSI or in a weighted gauge pressure canner at 10 pounds PSI.

8. Once completed, remove the canner from the heat. Carefully tilt the weight to make sure there is no more steam to escape before removing completely. Wait for 10 minutes, then carefully remove the lid.

9. Place the jars 1 inch apart on a clean towel, out of direct light, and leave undisturbed for at least 12 to 24 hours.

Great Northern Beans

YIELD: 8 (1-quart) jars | **PREP:** Active time, 1 hour 45 minutes / Inactive time, 1 hour 35 minutes

Great northern beans are also fondly referred to as navy beans, despite their bright white appearance. They earned this name because they were commonly served to U.S. soldiers as a war staple. These beans have a delicious mild and nutty flavor. They pair well with almost anything and are packed full of vitamins and fiber.

5 pounds dried great northern beans
2½ teaspoons salt

1. Sort through the dried beans and remove any stones or debris. Wash, rinse, and drain the beans.

2. In a large stockpot, combine the dried beans and enough water to cover by 2 inches. Bring to a boil and cook for 2 minutes.

3. Remove from the heat and let the beans soak for 1 hour.

4. Drain the beans and reserve the liquid for packing the jars.

5. Ladle the beans into hot jars. Cover with the reserved liquid, leaving 1 inch of headspace. Using the measurer, pop any air bubbles inside the jars and adjust the fill, if needed, to reach the proper headspace.

6. Dampen a corner of a paper towel with white vinegar and clean the jar rims. Place lids onto jars and, using a tea towel, lightly finger-tighten the bands onto the lids. Do not tighten past finger tight. Wipe jar rims to remove any oily residue.

7. Carefully lift the jars onto the rack in the canner without tilting the jars. Secure the lid onto the canner and heat the water to 180 degrees for Hot Pack recipes. Let the canner exhaust for 10 continuous minutes.

8. Place the pressure regulator or weighted gauge on the vent and process for 1 hour 15 minutes for quart jars in a dial gauge pressure canner at 11 pounds PSI or in a weighted gauge pressure canner at 10 pounds PSI.

9. Once completed, remove the canner from the heat. Carefully tilt the weight to make sure there is no more steam to escape before removing completely. Wait for 10 minutes, then carefully remove the lid.

10. Place the jars 1 inch apart on a clean towel, out of direct light, and leave undisturbed for at least 12 to 24 hours.

VARIATION TIP: The processing time for other types of dried beans of a similar size is the same. Try mixing it up and canning multiple beans for a 5- or 7-bean soup. Or replace the great northern beans with a favorite similar-size bean.

Zesty Black Beans

YIELD: 10 (1-pint) jars | **PREP:** Active time, 1 hour 45 minutes / Inactive time, 1 hour 25 minutes

Black beans are one of the best protein staples to have on hand. They are a great feature for meatless meals or Taco Tuesday with friends. The heat from the jalapeño and cayenne are balanced by the sugar and tomato juice. This versatile recipe can be prepared in bulk and used alongside a favorite meal.

3¼ pounds dried black beans

1 to 2 tablespoons olive oil

1 large yellow onion, chopped

1 jalapeño pepper, diced

¼ teaspoon dried cilantro

¼ teaspoon cayenne pepper

3 tablespoons sugar

2 teaspoons salt

1 (46-ounce) can tomato juice

1. Sort through the dried beans and remove any stones or debris. Wash, rinse, and drain the beans.

2. In a large stockpot, combine the dried beans and enough water to cover the beans by 2 inches. Cover, bring to a boil, and cook for 2 minutes.

3. Remove from the heat and let the beans soak for 1 hour.

4. Drain the beans and reserve the liquid for packing the jars. Remove the beans to a separate bowl and set aside.

5. Heat the stockpot over medium-high heat. Once hot, pour in the olive oil and heat until it is shimmering. Add the onion and jalapeño and cook until they soften and turn translucent, for about 5 minutes. Add the cilantro, cayenne, sugar, and salt. Cook for 1 minute, then add the tomato juice and beans and cook for 1 more minute. Remove from the heat.

6. Ladle the beans into hot jars, leaving 1 inch of headspace. Using the measurer, pop any air bubbles inside the jars and adjust the fill, if needed, to reach the proper headspace.

7. Dampen a corner of a paper towel with white vinegar and clean the jar rims. Place lids onto jars and, using a tea towel, lightly finger-tighten the bands onto the lids. Do not tighten past finger tight. Wipe jar rims to remove any oily residue.

8. Carefully lift the jars onto the rack in the canner without tilting the jars. Secure the lid onto the canner and heat the water to 180 degrees for Hot Pack recipes. Let the canner exhaust for 10 continuous minutes.

9. Place the pressure regulator or weighted gauge on the vent and process for 1 hour 5 minutes for pint jars in a dial gauge pressure canner at 11 pounds PSI or in a weighted gauge pressure canner at 10 pounds PSI.

10. Once completed, remove the canner from the heat. Carefully tilt the weight to make sure there is no more steam to escape before removing completely. Wait for 10 minutes, then carefully remove the lid.

11. Place the jars 1 inch apart on a clean towel, out of direct light, and leave undisturbed for at least 12 to 24 hours.

Herb Salted Tuna

YIELD: 6 (1-pint) jars | **PREP:** Active time, 10 minutes / Inactive time, 2 hours 30 minutes

When a lighter lunch or snack is desired, this tuna recipe is perfect. It's a low-fat, high-protein choice that can be eaten straight out of the jar, served on flavorful crackers with cucumbers and dill, or tossed with mayo for a satisfying tuna melt sandwich with fries.

4 to 6 pounds frozen tuna, thawed and skin tissue and dark sections removed, cut into 2-inch pieces

1½ teaspoons dried dill

1½ teaspoons dried rosemary

3 teaspoons salt, divided

Olive oil, for covering tuna in jars

1. Pack the tuna into jars, leaving 1 inch of head-space. Smaller pieces of tuna can be used to fill any gaps.

2. Combine the dried dill and rosemary in a small dish.

3. Season each jar of tuna with ½ teaspoon of salt and ¼ teaspoon of combined dried herbs. Add oil to cover tuna, leaving 1 inch of headspace. Using the measurer, pop any air bubbles inside the jars and adjust the fill, if needed, to reach the proper headspace.

4. Dampen a corner of a paper towel with white vinegar and clean the jar rims. Place lids onto jars and, using a tea towel, lightly finger-tighten the bands onto the lids. Do not tighten past finger tight. Wipe jar rims to remove any oily residue.

5. Carefully lift the jars onto the rack in the canner without tilting the jars. Secure the lid onto the canner and heat the water to 140 degrees for Raw Pack recipes. Let the canner exhaust for 10 continuous minutes.

6. Place the pressure regulator or weighted gauge on the vent and process for 1 hour 50 minutes for pint jars in a dial gauge pressure canner at 11 pounds PSI or in a weighted gauge pressure canner at 10 pounds PSI.

7. Once completed, remove the canner from the heat. Carefully tilt the weight to make sure there is no more steam to escape before removing completely. Wait for 10 minutes, then carefully remove the lid.

8. Place the jars 1 inch apart on a clean towel, out of direct light, and leave undisturbed for at least 12 to 24 hours.

INGREDIENT TIP: It's best to use frozen tuna that has been thawed. Crystals often form on canned tuna, and there is no way to prevent them from forming. These crystals are magnesium ammonium phosphate, which are naturally occurring mineral elements that come from the ocean where the fish lives. These crystals can look like glass or plastic; they typically dissolve when heated and are safe to consume.

Caramelized Onions

YIELD: 10 (1-pint) jars | **PREP:** Active time, 1 hour 10 minutes / Inactive time, 1 hour 35 minutes

Caramelized onions are one of those ingredients that pay dividends. They are ideal when made in bulk because they can be time consuming to prepare. Having these ready in the pantry is a game changer for flatbread pizza, for party dips, and as a topping on roasted meats.

5 tablespoons butter

10 pounds yellow onions, halved and sliced ¼ to ½ inch thick

1 teaspoon salt

½ cup brown sugar

¼ cup Worcestershire sauce

¼ cup molasses

1. Heat a stockpot over medium-high heat. Once the pot is hot, drop in the butter and cook until it starts to bubble. Add the onions and let them sit for about 5 minutes.

2. Reduce the heat to medium, stir, and let cook for another 5 minutes.

3. Add the salt and sugar, then stir. Be sure to let the onions sit without stirring too often so they have a chance to brown and darken, without sticking.

4. Add the Worcestershire sauce and scrape up any bits stuck to the bottom. Add the molasses and stir.

5. Continue cooking the onions for another hour, adjusting the heat lower if they start to stick. The onions should turn slightly jammy and dark brown but still retain their individual shape. Remove the onions from the heat.

6. Ladle the onions into hot jars, leaving 1 inch of headspace. Using the measurer, pop any air bubbles inside the jars and adjust the fill, if needed, to reach the proper headspace.

7. Dampen a corner of a paper towel with white vinegar and clean the jar rims. Place lids onto jars and, using a tea towel, lightly finger-tighten the bands onto the lids. Do not tighten past finger tight. Wipe jar rims to remove any oily residue.

8. Carefully lift the jars onto the rack in the canner without tilting the jars. Secure the lid onto the canner and heat the water to 180 degrees for Hot Pack recipes. Let the canner exhaust for 10 continuous minutes.

9. Place the pressure regulator or weighted gauge on the vent and process for 1 hour 15 minutes for pint jars in a dial gauge pressure canner at 11 pounds PSI or in a weighted gauge pressure canner at 10 pounds PSI.

10. Once completed, remove the canner from the heat. Carefully tilt the weight to make sure there is no more steam to escape before removing completely. Wait for 10 minutes, then carefully remove the lid.

11. Place the jars 1 inch apart on a clean towel, out of direct light, and leave undisturbed for at least 12 to 24 hours.

> **VARIATION TIP:** To make this recipe vegan, substitute avocado oil for the butter and a vegan Worcestershire for the Worcestershire sauce.

HOT PACK

Garlicky Dill Relish

YIELD: 7 (1-pint) jars | **PREP:** Active time, 30 minutes / Inactive time, 40 minutes

Garlic and dill are flavorful, bold, and complementary to one another. This relish is a snap to add to tuna salad, serve with your favorite crackers, or layer on a sandwich. This recipe packs flavor and will elevate any meal.

14 pounds cucumbers
1 large or 2 small bell peppers, red, green, or both
3 medium white or yellow onions
2 tablespoons fresh dill
2 tablespoons dill seed
4 cups apple cider vinegar
3 tablespoons mustard seeds
3 tablespoons minced garlic
½ cup pickling salt

1. Peel the cucumbers, cutting off the ends. Slice the cucumbers in half, then remove and discard the seeds. Cut the cucumbers into 1-inch pieces, then put in a food processor. Process until the cucumbers are in ¼-inch pieces or smaller. Once processed, remove the vegetables to a medium bowl and set aside.

2. Remove the stems, seeds, and ribs from the bell peppers. Cut the peppers into 1-inch pieces, then put in the food processor. Process until the peppers are in ¼-inch pieces or smaller. Once processed, remove the vegetables to a medium bowl and set aside.

3. Peel the onions, cut into quarters, and put in the food processor. Process until the onions are in ¼-inch pieces or smaller. Once processed, remove the vegetables to a medium bowl and set aside.

4. Combine the processed vegetables, dill, dill seed, vinegar, mustard seeds, garlic, and salt in a large stockpot and bring to a boil. Reduce the heat to a simmer and cook for 10 minutes. Remove from the heat.

5. Ladle the relish into hot jars, leaving ½ inch of headspace. Using the measurer, pop any air bubbles inside the jars and adjust the fill, if needed, to reach the proper headspace.

6. Dampen a corner of a paper towel with white vinegar and clean the jar rims. Place lids onto jars and, using a tea towel, lightly finger-tighten the bands onto the lids. Do not tighten past finger tight. Wipe jar rims to remove any oily residue.

7. Carefully lift the jars onto the rack in the canner without tilting the jars. Secure the lid onto the canner and heat the water to 180 degrees for Hot Pack recipes. Let the canner exhaust for 10 continuous minutes.

8. Place the pressure regulator or weighted gauge on the vent and process for 20 minutes for pint jars in a dial gauge pressure canner at 11 pounds PSI or in a weighted gauge pressure canner at 10 pounds PSI.

9. Once completed, remove the canner from the heat. Carefully tilt the weight to make sure there is no more steam to escape before removing completely. Wait for 10 minutes, then carefully remove the lid.

10. Place the jars 1 inch apart on a clean towel, out of direct light, and leave undisturbed for at least 12 to 24 hours.

HOT PACK

Fire-Roasted Tomato and Red Pepper Pesto

YIELD: 6 (1-pint) jars | **PREP:** Active time, 5 minutes / Inactive time, 55 minutes

Fire-roasted pesto adds a depth of flavor that transforms any dish. This pesto makes a great spread for panini or can be mixed in with pasta sauce for an extra savory boost. Take a spoonful and top a fried egg, or even mix into a batch of steamed rice to elevate any meal.

2 (28-ounce) cans fire-roasted tomatoes

16 ounces fire-roasted red peppers

4 garlic cloves, peeled

4 stems basil, leaves removed

1½ teaspoons salt

1. Put the tomatoes, red peppers, garlic, basil, and salt in a food processor and process until the desired consistency is reached.

2. Place the pesto in a large stockpot and bring to a boil, then remove from the heat.

3. Ladle the pesto into hot jars, leaving ½ inch of headspace. Using the measurer, pop any air bubbles inside the jars and adjust the fill, if needed, to reach the proper headspace.

4. Dampen a corner of a paper towel with white vinegar and clean the jar rims. Place lids onto jars and, using a tea towel, lightly finger-tighten the bands onto the lids. Do not tighten past finger tight. Wipe jar rims to remove any oily residue.

5. Carefully lift the jars onto the rack in the canner without tilting the jars. Secure the lid onto the canner and heat the water to 180 degrees for Hot Pack recipes. Let the canner exhaust for 10 continuous minutes.

6. Place the pressure regulator or weighted gauge on the vent and process for 35 minutes for pint jars in a dial gauge pressure canner at 11 pounds PSI or in a weighted gauge pressure canner at 10 pounds PSI.

7. Once completed, remove the canner from the heat. Carefully tilt the weight to make sure there is no more steam to escape before removing completely. Wait for 10 minutes, then carefully remove the lid.

8. Place the jars 1 inch apart on a clean towel, out of direct light, and leave undisturbed for at least 12 to 24 hours.

HOT PACK

Sweet and Smoky Barbecue Sauce

YIELD: 6 (1-pint) jars | **PREP:** Active time, 45 minutes / Inactive time, 55 minutes

This barbecue sauce is a great combination of smoky spices and sweet brown sugar that will make any cookout a hit. Slather this sauce on ribs or smoked chicken, or use for dipping with nuggets.

4 (28-ounce) cans tomato puree

1 yellow onion, chopped

2 celery stalks, chopped

2 green bell peppers with stems, seeds, and ribs removed, chopped

2 jalapeño peppers with stems, seeds, and ribs removed, chopped

1 cup brown sugar

1 cup apple cider vinegar

1 tablespoon dry mustard

1 tablespoon smoked paprika

¼ teaspoon cayenne pepper

1. In a large stockpot, combine the tomato puree, onion, celery, bell peppers, jalapeños, brown sugar, vinegar, mustard, paprika, and cayenne. Bring to a boil, then reduce the heat and simmer for 30 minutes. Remove from the heat.

2. Puree the ingredients in a food processor or with an immersion blender until the desired texture has been reached. Strain the sauce, if desired.

3. Ladle the sauce into hot jars, leaving ½ inch of headspace. Using the measurer, pop any air bubbles inside the jars and adjust the fill, if needed, to reach the proper headspace.

4. Dampen a corner of a paper towel with white vinegar and clean the jar rims. Place lids onto jars and, using a tea towel, lightly finger-tighten the bands onto the lids. Do not tighten past finger tight. Wipe jar rims to remove any oily residue.

5. Carefully lift the jars onto the rack in the canner without tilting the jars. Secure the lid onto the canner and heat the water to 180 degrees for Hot Pack recipes. Let the canner exhaust for 10 continuous minutes.

6. Place the pressure regulator or weighted gauge on the vent and process for 35 minutes for pint jars in a dial gauge pressure canner at 11 pounds PSI or in a weighted gauge pressure canner at 10 pounds PSI.

7. Once completed, remove the canner from the heat. Carefully tilt the weight to make sure there is no more steam to escape before removing completely. Wait for 10 minutes, then carefully remove the lid.

8. Place the jars 1 inch apart on a clean towel, out of direct light, and leave undisturbed for at least 12 to 24 hours.

Apple Honey Butter

YIELD: 6 (1-pint) jars | **PREP:** Active time, 30 minutes / Inactive time, 1 hour 35 minutes

This autumnal recipe will bring to mind pumpkin patches, hayrides, and crisp sweater weather. It's best served spread on a favorite soft bread or pastry. Mix it up using pumpkin pie spice, brown sugar, or maple syrup instead of honey.

5 pounds apples, a variety of sweet and tart, peeled, cored, and chopped
2 cups apple cider
2 teaspoons cinnamon
1 teaspoon nutmeg
¼ teaspoon ground cloves
1 cup sugar
1 cup honey
2 teaspoons salt

1. In a large stockpot, combine the apples, cider, cinnamon, nutmeg, cloves, and sugar and bring to a boil. Cover with a lid and simmer for 1 hour.

2. Remove from the heat and process the ingredients with an immersion blender or in batches in a regular blender.

3. Add the honey and salt to the stockpot and bring to a simmer, then cook until the butter reaches the desired consistency. Remove from the heat.

4. Ladle the butter into hot jars, leaving ¼ inch of headspace. Using the measurer, pop any air bubbles inside the jar and adjust the fill, if needed, to reach the proper headspace.

5. Dampen a corner of a paper towel with white vinegar and clean the jar rims. Place lids onto jars and, using a tea towel, lightly finger-tighten the bands onto the lids. Do not tighten past finger tight. Wipe jar rims to remove any oily residue.

6. Carefully lift the jars onto the rack in the canner without tilting the jars. Secure the lid onto the canner and heat the water to 180 degrees for Hot Pack recipes. Let the canner exhaust for 10 continuous minutes.

7. Place the pressure regulator or weighted gauge on the vent and process for 15 minutes for pint jars in a dial gauge pressure canner at 11 pounds PSI or in a weighted gauge pressure canner at 10 pounds PSI.

8. Once completed, remove the canner from the heat. Carefully tilt the weight to make sure there is no more steam to escape before removing completely. Wait for 10 minutes, then carefully remove the lid.

9. Place the jars 1 inch apart on a clean towel, out of direct light, and leave undisturbed for at least 12 to 24 hours.

Chocolate-Strawberry Sauce

YIELD: 6 (1-pint) jars | **PREP:** Active time, 30 minutes / Inactive time, 35 minutes

These blended strawberries become so decadent with the addition of cocoa powder. This flavorful yumminess can be drizzled on morning waffles, marshmallows, or a favorite dessert.

3 quarts fresh or frozen strawberries (thawed thoroughly if using frozen), hulled and leaves removed

1 cup lemon juice

2 cups unsweetened cocoa powder

8 cups sugar

1 cup Clear Jel, less or more depending on the desired thickness of the syrup

1. Put the strawberries in a large stockpot and process with an immersion blender or regular blender until the desired consistency is reached. Heat over medium-high heat.

2. Add the lemon juice, cocoa powder, and sugar. If the strawberries do not release enough juice, add ¼ cup of water, or more, to reach the desired consistency. Add the Clear Jel and bring to a boil. Let the sauce boil for 1 minute, stirring occasionally, then remove from the heat.

3. Ladle the sauce into hot jars, leaving ½ inch of headspace. Using the measurer, pop any air bubbles inside the jars and adjust the fill, if needed, to reach the proper headspace.

4. Dampen a corner of a paper towel with white vinegar and clean the jar rims. Place lids onto jars and, using a tea towel, lightly finger-tighten the bands onto the lids. Do not tighten past finger tight. Wipe jar rims to remove any oily residue.

5. Carefully lift the jars onto the rack in the canner without tilting the jars. Secure the lid onto the canner and heat the water to 180 degrees for Hot Pack recipes. Let the canner exhaust for 10 continuous minutes.

6. Place the pressure regulator or weighted gauge on the vent and process for 15 minutes for pint jars in a dial gauge pressure canner at 11 pounds PSI or in a weighted gauge pressure canner at 10 pounds PSI.

7. Once completed, remove the canner from the heat. Carefully tilt the weight to make sure there is no more steam to escape before removing completely. Wait for 10 minutes, then carefully remove the lid.

8. Place the jars 1 inch apart on a clean towel, out of direct light, and leave undisturbed for at least 12 to 24 hours.

VARIATION TIP: Swap out the strawberries for fresh raspberries when in season.

**Hearty Stewed
Beef** 88

Stocks, Soups, and Stews

Mighty Bone Broth

YIELD: 10 (1-pint) jars | **PREP:** Active time, 1 to 4 hours / Inactive time, 40 minutes

Bone broth has been a hit for many years, and this recipe is the best. It incorporates marrow bones, fresh herbs, and eggshells to develop a delicious liquid that also packs a nutritious punch. This broth is amazing in soups, stews, rice, or polenta or simply to sip in place of a morning coffee.

1 pound marrow bones

2 to 3 eggshells, rinsed

1 celery stalk with leaves, chopped

1 yellow onion, quartered

1 tablespoon salt

½ tablespoon fresh oregano

1 large garlic clove, smashed

1 knob fresh turmeric, about 1 inch, sliced

1 knob fresh ginger, about 1 inch, sliced

½ teaspoon freshly ground black pepper or cayenne pepper (optional)

1. In a large stockpot, combine the marrow bones, eggshells, celery, onion, salt, oregano, garlic, turmeric, ginger, and pepper (if using). Cover the ingredients with water, leaving at least 1 inch of space, and cover with a lid. Bring to a boil for 1 minute, then reduce the heat and simmer for 1 to 4 hours.

2. Check the broth regularly and add water to keep the soup covered if it cooks down. Skim off any foam that appears on the surface and discard. Taste the broth often and adjust seasonings accordingly.

3. Remove the broth from the heat and let it cool slightly. Strain the contents. Let the broth continue to cool, then skim the top with a spoon, removing any fat. Reheat the broth until boiling. Remove from the heat.

4. Ladle the broth into hot jars, leaving 1 inch of headspace. Using the measurer, pop any air bubbles inside the jars and adjust the fill, if needed, to reach the proper headspace.

5. Dampen a corner of a paper towel with white vinegar and clean the jar rims. Place lids onto jars and, using a tea towel, lightly finger-tighten the bands onto the lids. Do not tighten past finger tight. Wipe jar rims to remove any oily residue.

6. Carefully lift the jars onto the rack in the canner without tilting the jars. Secure the lid onto the canner and heat the water to 180 degrees for Hot Pack recipes. Let the canner exhaust for 10 continuous minutes.

7. Place the pressure regulator or weighted gauge on the vent and process for 20 minutes for pint jars in a dial gauge pressure canner at 11 pounds PSI or in a weighted gauge pressure canner at 10 pounds PSI.

8. Once completed, remove the canner from the heat. Carefully tilt the weight to make sure there is no more steam to escape before removing completely. Wait for 10 minutes, then carefully remove the lid.

9. Place the jars 1 inch apart on a clean towel, out of direct light, and leave undisturbed for at least 12 to 24 hours.

> **VARIATION TIP:** Alternatively, this can be prepared in a slow cooker overnight on low for 8 to 12 hours.

Savory Vegetable Broth

YIELD: 10 (1-pint) jars | **PREP:** Active time, 1 to 4 hours / Inactive time, 40 minutes

The tomato paste in this recipe adds warmth and a beautiful hue. This versatile broth is great in place of water when cooking rice or as a base for stews and soups.

1 pint Baby Bella
   mushrooms, sliced

2 large carrots,
   chopped

2 celery stalks with
   leaves, chopped

2 yellow onions,
   quartered

¼ cup tomato paste

½ tablespoon fresh
   oregano

½ tablespoon fresh
   thyme

1 large bay leaf

4 stems dandelion
   greens

2 large garlic cloves

1 tablespoon salt

½ teaspoon freshly
   ground black pepper
   or cayenne pepper
   (optional)

1. In a large stockpot, combine the mushrooms, carrots, celery, onions, tomato paste, oregano, thyme, bay leaf, dandelion greens, garlic, salt, and pepper (if using). Cover the ingredients with cold water, leaving at least 1 inch of space, then cover with a lid. Bring to a boil for 1 minute, then reduce the heat and simmer for 1 to 4 hours.

2. Check the broth regularly and add water to keep the ingredients covered if it cooks down. Skim off any foam that appears on the surface and discard. Taste the broth often and adjust seasonings accordingly.

3. Remove the broth from the heat and let it cool slightly. Strain the contents. Let the broth continue to cool, then skim the top with a spoon, removing any fat. Reheat the broth until boiling. Remove from the heat.

4. Ladle the broth into hot jars, leaving 1 inch of headspace. Using the measurer, pop any air bubbles inside the jars and adjust the fill, if needed, to reach the proper headspace.

5. Dampen a corner of a paper towel with white vinegar and clean the jar rims. Place lids onto jars and, using a tea towel, lightly finger-tighten the bands onto the lids. Do not tighten past finger tight. Wipe jar rims to remove any oily residue.

6. Carefully lift the jars onto the rack in the canner without tilting the jars. Secure the lid onto the canner and heat the water to 180 degrees for Hot Pack recipes. Let the canner exhaust for 10 continuous minutes.

7. Place the pressure regulator or weighted gauge on the vent and process for 20 minutes for pint jars in a dial gauge pressure canner at 11 pounds PSI or in a weighted gauge pressure canner at 10 pounds PSI.

8. Once completed, remove the canner from the heat. Carefully tilt the weight to make sure there is no more steam to escape before removing completely. Wait for 10 minutes, then carefully remove the lid.

9. Place the jars 1 inch apart on a clean towel, out of direct light, and leave undisturbed for at least 12 to 24 hours.

VARIATION TIP: Alternatively, this can be prepared in a slow cooker overnight on low for 8 to 12 hours.

White Bean and Mushroom Soup

YIELD: 7 (1-quart) jars | **PREP:** Active time, 1 hour 30 minutes / Inactive time, 1 hour 50 minutes

This soup is incredibly comforting. And because we only fill the jars halfway with beans, it creates a good amount of delicious broth that can be used as a base for other soups or to layer on when preparing this to serve. Try adding bacon or smoked ham and serving with buttered corn bread for a delicious meal.

2½ pounds dried Great Northern Beans
2 tablespoons olive oil
1 pint Baby Bella mushrooms, sliced
1 large yellow or white onion, diced
2 garlic cloves, minced
2 fresh thyme sprigs, stemmed
1½ teaspoons salt
½ teaspoon freshly ground black pepper

1. In a large stockpot, combine the dried beans and enough water to cover by 2 inches. Cover and bring to a boil for 2 minutes, remove from the heat, and let the beans soak for 1 hour.

2. While the beans are soaking, heat a skillet over medium-high heat. Once the skillet is hot, pour in the oil and heat until shimmering. Add the mushrooms and onion and cook until they start browning. Add the garlic and cook for 1 minute. Season with the thyme, salt, and pepper and remove from the heat.

3. Drain the beans. Cover the beans in fresh water, then bring to a boil. Remove from the heat and drain the beans, reserving the liquid for packing the jars.

4. Fill hot jars halfway with the cooked beans. Layer the mushroom and onion mixture on top of the beans, distributing evenly between the jars. Fill jars with the reserved liquid, leaving 1 inch of headspace. Using the measurer, pop any air bubbles inside the jars and adjust the fill, if needed, to reach the proper headspace.

5. Dampen a corner of a paper towel with white vinegar and clean the jar rims. Place lids onto jars and, using a tea towel, lightly finger-tighten the bands onto the lids. Do not tighten past finger tight. Wipe jar rims to remove any oily residue.

6. Carefully lift the jars onto the rack in the canner without tilting the jars. Secure the lid onto the canner and heat the water to 180 degrees for Hot Pack recipes. Let the canner exhaust for 10 continuous minutes.

7. Place the pressure regulator or weighted gauge on the vent and process for 1 hour 30 minutes for quart jars in a dial gauge pressure canner at 11 pounds PSI or in a weighted gauge pressure canner at 10 pounds PSI.

8. Once completed, remove the canner from the heat. Carefully tilt the weight to make sure there is no more steam to escape before removing completely. Wait for 10 minutes, then carefully remove the lid.

9. Place the jars 1 inch apart on a clean towel, out of direct light, and leave undisturbed for at least 12 to 24 hours.

Dill Chicken Soup

YIELD: 4 (1-quart) jars | **PREP:** Active time, 20 minutes / Inactive time, 1 hour 10 minutes

It is important not to add noodles, rice, or any other thickeners when pressure canning. Alternatively, heat the pressure canned soup and cook pasta noodles or rice separately when ready to serve. This dish works great with orzo or even dumplings depending on the weather.

2 tablespoons olive oil, divided

2 large yellow onions, diced

2 cups thinly sliced carrots

2 cups thinly sliced celery

4 pounds boneless, skinless chicken breast, cut into 1-inch pieces

4 teaspoons salt

1½ teaspoons freshly ground black pepper

2 cups frozen green peas

¼ cup fresh dill, chopped

4 quarts chicken or vegetable broth

1. Heat a skillet over medium-high heat. Add 1 tablespoon of olive oil and heat until shimmering.

2. Add the onions, carrots, and celery and cook until the carrots are tender, for 4 to 5 minutes. Remove from the heat, transfer to a separate dish, and set aside.

3. Heat a large stockpot over medium-high heat. Add the remaining 1 tablespoon of olive oil and let it heat until shimmering. Add the chicken, salt, and pepper. Let the chicken sear on each side for 1 to 2 minutes, or until golden brown.

4. Keep the heat on medium-high. Once the chicken has been seared on all sides, add the onions, carrots, and celery to the stockpot. Add the green peas and dill, letting the ingredients cook together for 1 minute. Add the broth and bring to a boil over high heat. Once boiling, turn off the heat.

5. Ladle the soup into hot jars, leaving 1 inch of headspace. Using the measurer, pop any air bubbles inside the jars and adjust the fill, if needed, to reach the proper headspace.

6. Dampen a corner of a paper towel with white vinegar and clean the jar rims. Place lids onto jars and, using a tea towel, lightly finger-tighten the bands onto the lids. Do not tighten past finger tight. Wipe jar rims to remove any oily residue.

7. Carefully lift the jars onto the rack in the canner without tilting the jars. Secure the lid onto the canner and heat the water to 180 degrees for Hot Pack recipes. Let the canner exhaust for 10 continuous minutes.

8. Place the pressure regulator or weighted gauge on the vent and process for 1 hour 10 minutes for quart jars in a dial gauge pressure canner at 11 pounds PSI or in a weighted gauge pressure canner at 10 pounds PSI.

9. Once completed, remove the canner from the heat. Carefully tilt the weight to make sure there is no more steam to escape before removing completely. Wait for 10 minutes, then carefully remove the lid.

10. Place the jars 1 inch apart on a clean towel, out of direct light, and leave undisturbed for at least 12 to 24 hours.

Chicken Enchilada Soup

YIELD: 4 (1-quart) jars | **PREP:** Active time, 30 minutes / Inactive time, 1 hour 20 minutes

Try this soup garnished with lime, cilantro, avocado, and crushed corn chips. To thicken, whisk a little water into corn flour to make a slurry, then add to the soup.

2 teaspoons olive oil

2½ pounds boneless, skinless chicken breast, cut into 1-inch pieces

1 large yellow onion, diced

1 jalapeño pepper, diced

1 (15-ounce) can red enchilada sauce

1 (15-ounce) can black beans, drained

1 (15-ounce) can corn, drained

1 (15-ounce) can diced tomatoes with green chiles

2 teaspoons chili powder

1 teaspoon ground cumin

1 teaspoon dried oregano leaves

4 quarts chicken broth

1. Heat a large stockpot over medium-high heat. Once the pot is hot, add the olive oil and heat until shimmering. Once shimmering, add the chicken and sear on each side until golden brown. Add the onion and jalapeño and continue cooking for 1 to 2 minutes, or until the vegetables start to soften.

2. Add the enchilada sauce, beans, corn, tomatoes and chiles, chili powder, cumin, and oregano and cook for 1 minute.

3. Cover with the broth and bring to a boil. Once boiling, reduce the heat and simmer for 15 minutes. Remove from the heat.

4. Ladle the soup into hot jars, leaving 1 inch of headspace. Using the measurer, pop any air bubbles inside the jars and adjust the fill, if needed, to reach the proper headspace.

5. Dampen a corner of a paper towel with white vinegar and clean the jar rims. Place lids onto jars and, using a tea towel, lightly finger-tighten the bands onto the lids. Do not tighten past finger tight. Wipe jar rims to remove any oily residue.

6. Carefully lift the jars onto the rack in the canner without tilting the jars. Secure the lid onto the canner and heat the water to 180 degrees for Hot Pack recipes. Let the canner exhaust for 10 continuous minutes.

7. Place the pressure regulator or weighted gauge on the vent and process for 1 hour for pint jars in a dial gauge pressure canner at 11 pounds PSI or in a weighted gauge pressure canner at 10 pounds PSI.

8. Once completed, remove the canner from the heat. Carefully tilt the weight to make sure there is no more steam to escape before removing completely. Wait for 10 minutes, then carefully remove the lid.

9. Place the jars 1 inch apart on a clean towel, out of direct light, and leave undisturbed for at least 12 to 24 hours.

Zesty Tortilla-Less Chicken Soup

YIELD: 8 (1-pint) jars | **PREP:** Active time, 40 minutes / Inactive time, 1 hour 20 minutes

A flavorful treat, this can be served with shredded cheese, sour cream, lime, and steamed flour tortillas. A flavorful treat, this can be served with shredded cheese, sour cream, lime, and steamed flour tortillas. Try panfrying corn tortilla strips and topping your soup for an added crunch.

2 teaspoons olive oil

2½ pounds boneless, skinless chicken breasts, cut into 1-inch pieces

1 tablespoon salt, divided

1 large yellow onion, diced

2 garlic cloves, minced

2 tablespoons chili powder

1 tablespoon ground cumin

¼ cup cilantro, chopped

30 ounces diced tomatoes with green chiles

Zest and juice of 1 lime

3 quarts chicken broth or stock

1. Heat a large stockpot over medium high-heat. Once hot, pour in the oil and heat until shimmering. Add the chicken and cook until golden brown. Season the chicken with 2 teaspoons of salt. Remove from the heat.

2. Add the onion and cook until tender, for 4 to 5 minutes. Add the garlic and cook for 1 minute.

3. Add the chili powder, cumin, cilantro, tomatoes and chiles, lime zest and juice, and the remaining 1 teaspoon of salt, then cook for 1 minute.

4. Add the broth and bring to a boil. Once boiling, reduce the heat and let simmer for 15 minutes. Remove from the heat.

5. Pack the chicken evenly into hot jars. Then, ladle the soup over the chicken, leaving 1 inch of headspace. Using the measurer, pop any air bubbles inside the jars and adjust the fill, if needed, to reach the proper headspace.

6. Dampen a corner of a paper towel with white vinegar and clean the jar rims. Place lids onto jars and, using a tea towel, lightly finger-tighten

the bands onto the lids. Do not tighten past finger tight. Wipe jar rims to remove any oily residue.

7. Carefully lift the jars onto the rack in the canner without tilting the jars. Secure the lid onto the canner and heat the water to 180 degrees for Hot Pack recipes. Let the canner exhaust for 10 continuous minutes.

8. Place the pressure regulator or weighted gauge on the vent and process for 1 hour for pint jars in a dial gauge pressure canner at 11 pounds PSI or in a weighted gauge pressure canner at 10 pounds PSI.

9. Once completed, remove the canner from the heat. Carefully tilt the weight to make sure there is no more steam to escape before removing completely. Wait for 10 minutes, then carefully remove the lid.

10. Place the jars 1 inch apart on a clean towel, out of direct light, and leave undisturbed for at least 12 to 24 hours.

HOT PACK

Kimchi Soup

YIELD: 8 (1-pint) jars | **PREP:** Active time, 30 minutes / Inactive time, 1 hour 35 minutes

Kimchi soup is a favorite for so many people. Known as kimchi stew, or kimchi jjigae, it is warm, spicy, and full of vegetables. Be versatile in garnishing this soup by serving it with fresh greens, crispy fried mushrooms, pork belly, or seared tofu.

2 teaspoons olive oil

1½ pounds boneless pork ribs, cut into 1-inch pieces

3 cups sour kimchi, with liquid

3 scallions, thinly sliced (use the entire scallion with ends trimmed)

3 tablespoons miso paste

3 tablespoons soy sauce

1 teaspoon crushed red pepper flakes

½ teaspoon salt

½ teaspoon freshly ground black pepper

4 cups mushroom broth

1. Heat a large stockpot over medium-high heat. Once the stockpot is hot, pour in the oil and heat until shimmering. Add the pork and sear until golden brown.

2. Add the kimchi with liquid, scallions, miso paste, soy sauce, and red pepper flakes and cook together for 1 to 2 minutes.

3. Add the salt, pepper, and mushroom broth. Add water to cover the ingredients by 2 inches. Bring the soup to a boil, then reduce the heat and let the soup simmer for 15 minutes. Remove from the heat.

4. Ladle the soup into hot jars, leaving 1 inch of headspace. Using the measurer, pop any air bubbles inside the jars and adjust the fill, if needed, to reach the proper headspace.

5. Dampen a corner of a paper towel with white vinegar and clean the jar rims. Place lids onto jars and, using a tea towel, lightly finger-tighten the bands onto the lids. Do not tighten past finger tight. Wipe jar rims to remove any oily residue.

6. Carefully lift the jars onto the rack in the canner without tilting the jars. Secure the lid onto the canner and heat the water to 180 degrees for Hot Pack recipes. Let the canner exhaust for 10 continuous minutes.

7. Place the pressure regulator or weighted gauge on the vent and process for 1 hour 15 minutes for pint jars in a dial gauge pressure canner at 11 pounds PSI or in a weighted gauge pressure canner at 10 pounds PSI.

8. Once completed, remove the canner from the heat. Carefully tilt the weight to make sure there is no more steam to escape before removing completely. Wait for 10 minutes, then carefully remove the lid.

9. Place the jars 1 inch apart on a clean towel, out of direct light, and leave undisturbed for at least 12 to 24 hours.

HOT PACK

Sausage, Kale, and Sweet Potato Soup

YIELD: 8 (1-pint) jars | **PREP:** Active time, 30 minutes / Inactive time, 1 hour 20 minutes

This soup is delicious served as is, but to make it creamier, once the soup is ready to serve, add heavy cream to the pot until the desired consistency is reached, remove from the heat, then stir to combine.

2 teaspoons olive oil

4 pounds ground spicy or hot pork sausage

3 bunches curly kale, stemmed and chopped

3 large sweet potatoes, peeled and cut into ½-inch cubes

2 teaspoons salt

2 to 3 quarts vegetable broth or water

1. Heat a large stockpot over medium-high heat. Once hot, add the oil and heat until shimmering. Start browning the sausage, for 3 to 4 minutes per side. Roughly break up the sausage into bite-size pieces as it browns. Place on paper towels to absorb some of the fat.

2. Add the kale to the stockpot and let it cook for 1 minute. It will reduce in size by about half. Add the sweet potatoes, salt, broth, and sausage, bringing the soup to a boil. Once boiling, reduce the heat and let simmer for 15 minutes. Remove from the heat.

3. Ladle the soup into hot jars, leaving 1 inch of headspace. Using the measurer, pop any air bubbles inside the jars and adjust the fill, if needed, to reach the proper headspace.

4. Dampen a corner of a paper towel with white vinegar and clean the jar rims. Place lids onto jars and, using a tea towel, lightly finger-tighten the bands onto the lids. Do not tighten past finger tight. Wipe jar rims to remove any oily residue.

5. Carefully lift the jars onto the rack in the canner without tilting the jars. Secure the lid onto the canner and heat the water to 180 degrees for Hot Pack recipes. Let the canner exhaust for 10 continuous minutes.

6. Place the pressure regulator or weighted gauge on the vent and process for 1 hour for pint jars in a dial gauge pressure canner at 11 pounds PSI or in a weighted gauge pressure canner at 10 pounds PSI.

7. Once completed, remove the canner from the heat. Carefully tilt the weight to make sure there is no more steam to escape before removing completely. Wait for 10 minutes, then carefully remove the lid.

8. Place the jars 1 inch apart on a clean towel, out of direct light, and leave undisturbed for at least 12 to 24 hours.

VARIATION TIP: This recipe also works well with Yukon Gold or red potatoes instead of the sweet potatoes.

Turkey, Sweet Potato, and Bean Chili

YIELD: 10 (1-pint) jars | **PREP:** Active time, 35 minutes / Inactive time, 1 hour 35 minutes

Add sweet potato to any chili for the best game-day comfort food, and start with this turkey chili recipe. This leaner version is incredibly satisfying and delicious. Don't be surprised when people ask for a second serving. Serve with corn chips, Greek yogurt, and hot sauce.

3 tablespoons olive oil

2 pounds ground turkey

5 teaspoons salt, divided

3 large sweet potatoes, peeled and cut into ½-inch cubes

2 large yellow onions, chopped

2 tablespoons paprika

1 tablespoon cumin

1 teaspoon cayenne pepper (optional)

30 ounces canned black beans, drained

30 ounces canned kidney beans, drained

3 quarts chicken broth or stock

1. Heat a large stockpot over medium-high heat. Once hot, pour in the oil and heat until shimmering. Start browning the ground turkey, for 3 to 4 minutes per side. Season the turkey with 2 teaspoons of salt. Roughly break up the turkey into bite-size pieces as it browns. Remove the turkey from the pan, and set aside.

2. Add the sweet potatoes to the stockpot and let them start to brown, for about 5 minutes. Add the onions, paprika, cumin, and cayenne (if using) and cook for 1 minute, letting the spices bloom. Add the black beans, kidney beans, remaining 3 teaspoons of salt, and the broth, then bring to a boil.

3. Add the turkey back to stockpot and reduce the heat, then let the soup simmer for 15 minutes. Remove from the heat.

4. Ladle the soup into hot jars, leaving 1 inch of headspace. Using the measurer, pop any air bubbles inside the jars and adjust the fill, if needed, to reach the proper headspace.

5. Dampen a corner of a paper towel with white vinegar and clean the jar rims. Place lids onto jars and, using a tea towel, lightly finger-tighten the bands onto the lids. Do not tighten past finger tight. Wipe jar rims to remove any oily residue.

6. Carefully lift the jars onto the rack in the canner without tilting the jars. Secure the lid onto the canner and heat the water to 180 degrees for Hot Pack recipes. Let the canner exhaust for 10 continuous minutes.

7. Place the pressure regulator or weighted gauge on the vent and process for 1 hour 15 minutes for pint jars in a dial gauge pressure canner at 11 pounds PSI or in a weighted gauge pressure canner at 10 pounds PSI.

8. Once completed, remove the canner from the heat. Carefully tilt the weight to make sure there is no more steam to escape before removing completely. Wait for 10 minutes, then carefully remove the lid.

9. Place the jars 1 inch apart on a clean towel, out of direct light, and leave undisturbed for at least 12 to 24 hours.

Lamb and Stout Stew

YIELD: 10 (1-pint) jars | **PREP:** Active time, 1 hour / Inactive time, 1 hour 35 minutes

The stout in this stew is important for flavor. Note that the alcohol will cook off in the preparation process. If you prefer not to use stout beer, replace it with broth or stock.

3 tablespoons olive oil

3 to 4 pounds lamb leg or shoulder, boned and cut into 1- to 1½-inch pieces

4 teaspoons salt, divided

2 teaspoons freshly ground black pepper, divided

3 pounds red or new potatoes, peeled and cut in half

2 large yellow onions, chopped

2 pounds carrots, chopped into ½-inch pieces

3 celery stalks, cut into ¼-inch slices

2 bay leaves

16 ounces stout beer

3 quarts beef broth or stock

1 pound green peas

1. Heat a large stockpot over medium-high heat. Once hot, pour in the oil and heat until shimmering. Season the lamb with 2 teaspoons of salt and 1 teaspoon of pepper. Once the oil is hot, start browning the lamb pieces in a single layer until browned on each side, for 2 to 3 minutes. This will take several batches. Be sure not to overcrowd the stockpot to avoid steaming the meat. Set the browned lamb aside.

2. Add the potatoes, onions, carrots, celery, bay leaves, stout, and broth to the stockpot over high heat and bring to a boil. Once boiling, reduce the heat, add the peas and the remaining 2 teaspoons of salt and 1 teaspoon of pepper, then simmer for 15 minutes. Remove the bay leaves and remove from the heat.

3. Portion the browned lamb into hot jars, evenly distributing the meat. Ladle the rest of the stew on top of the lamb, leaving 1 inch of headspace. Using the measurer, pop any air bubbles inside the jars and adjust the fill, if needed, to reach the proper headspace.

4. Dampen a corner of a paper towel with white vinegar and clean the jar rims. Place lids onto jars and, using a tea towel, lightly finger-tighten the bands onto the lids. Do not tighten past finger tight. Wipe jar rims to remove any oily residue.

5. Carefully lift the jars onto the rack in the canner without tilting the jars. Secure the lid onto the canner and heat the water to 180 degrees for Hot Pack recipes. Let the canner exhaust for 10 continuous minutes.

6. Place the pressure regulator or weighted gauge on the vent and process for 1 hour 15 minutes for pint jars in a dial gauge pressure canner at 11 pounds PSI or in a weighted gauge pressure canner at 10 pounds PSI.

7. Once completed, remove the canner from the heat. Carefully tilt the weight to make sure there is no more steam to escape before removing completely. Wait for 10 minutes, then carefully remove the lid.

8. Place the jars 1 inch apart on a clean towel, out of direct light, and leave undisturbed for at least 12 to 24 hours.

HOT PACK

Hearty Stewed Beef

YIELD: 10 (1-pint) jars | **PREP:** Active time, 1 hour / Inactive time, 1 hour 35 minutes

A hearty beef stew ready at your fingertips is one of the greatest rewards of pressure canning. Be sure not to add any thickeners, like flour, while browning the meat, as this can impact the effectiveness of pressure canning. The starchiness from the potatoes does a great job of creating a thick, stewed texture that will stick to your ribs. When you're ready to eat, serve topped with fresh parsley.

3 tablespoons olive oil

4 pounds beef chuck steak, cut into 1-inch pieces

4 teaspoons salt, divided

2 teaspoons freshly ground black pepper, divided (optional)

2 large yellow onions, chopped

4 large baking potatoes, peeled and cut into 1-inch pieces

2 to 3 pounds carrots, peeled and cut into ½-inch coins

3 celery stalks, cut into ¼-inch slices

28 ounces diced tomatoes

¾ teaspoon dried thyme

¾ teaspoon dried rosemary

3 quarts beef stock or broth

1. Heat a large stockpot over medium-high heat. Once hot, pour in the oil and heat until shimmering. Season the beef with 2 teaspoons of salt and 1 teaspoon of pepper (if using). Once the oil is hot, start browning the beef pieces in a single layer until browned on each side, for 2 to 3 minutes. This will take several batches. Be sure not to overcrowd the stockpot to avoid steaming the beef. Set the browned beef aside.

2. Add the onions, potatoes, carrots, celery, tomatoes, thyme, rosemary, and beef stock to the stockpot over high heat and bring to a boil. Once boiling, reduce the heat, add the remaining 2 teaspoons of salt and 1 teaspoon of pepper (if using), and simmer for 15 minutes. Remove from the heat.

3. Portion the browned beef into hot jars, evenly distributing the meat. Ladle the rest of the stew on top of the beef, leaving 1 inch of headspace. Using the measurer, pop any air bubbles inside the jars and adjust the fill, if needed, to reach the proper headspace.

4. Dampen a corner of a paper towel with white vinegar and clean the jar rims. Place lids onto jars and, using a tea towel, lightly finger-tighten the bands onto the lids. Do not tighten past finger tight. Wipe jar rims to remove any oily residue.

5. Carefully lift the jars onto the rack in the canner without tilting the jars. Secure the lid onto the canner and heat the water to 180 degrees for Hot Pack recipes. Let the canner exhaust for 10 continuous minutes.

6. Place the pressure regulator or weighted gauge on the vent and process for 1 hour 15 minutes for pint jars in a dial gauge pressure canner at 11 pounds PSI or in a weighted gauge pressure canner at 10 pounds PSI.

7. Once completed, remove the canner from the heat. Carefully tilt the weight to make sure there is no more steam to escape before removing completely. Wait for 10 minutes, then carefully remove the lid.

8. Place the jars 1 inch apart on a clean towel, out of direct light, and leave undisturbed for at least 12 to 24 hours.

All-Purpose Canned
Chicken 92

CHAPTER 5

Poultry, Meat, and Game

All-Purpose Canned Chicken

YIELD: 8 (1-quart) jars | **PREP:** Active time, 15 minutes / Inactive time, 1 hour 50 minutes

This canned chicken has a lightly seasoned flavor, which makes it convenient to add into other dishes. Try it in chicken salad, added to soups, filling enchiladas, or as a quick addition to taco night.

7 teaspoons salt
¼ teaspoon dried sage
¼ teaspoon dried rosemary
¼ teaspoon dried thyme
¼ teaspoon dried paprika
¼ teaspoon onion powder
¼ teaspoon garlic powder
¼ teaspoon dried parsley
12 to 15 pounds boneless, skinless chicken breasts or thighs, cut into 2-inch pieces

1. In a small bowl, combine the salt, sage, rosemary, thyme, paprika, onion powder, garlic powder, and parsley.

2. Heat a kettle of water until boiling, then remove from the heat.

3. Portion the raw chicken into jars, leaving 1¼ inch of headspace. Add 1 teaspoon of herbs and ½ inch of hot water to each jar. Using the measurer, pop any air bubbles inside the jars and adjust the fill, if needed, to reach the proper headspace.

4. Dampen a corner of a paper towel with white vinegar and clean the jar rims. Place lids onto jars and, using a tea towel, lightly finger-tighten the bands onto the lids. Do not tighten past finger tight. Wipe jar rims to remove any oily residue.

5. Carefully lift the jars onto the rack in the canner without tilting the jars. Secure the lid onto the canner and heat the water to 140 degrees for Raw Pack recipes. Let the canner exhaust for 10 continuous minutes.

6. Place the pressure regulator or weighted gauge on the vent and process for 1 hour 30 minutes for pint jars in a dial gauge pressure canner at 11 pounds PSI or in a weighted gauge pressure canner at 10 pounds PSI.

7. Once completed, remove the canner from the heat. Carefully tilt the weight to make sure there is no more steam to escape before removing completely. Wait for 10 minutes, then carefully remove the lid.

8. Place the jars 1 inch apart on a clean towel, out of direct light, and leave undisturbed for at least 12 to 24 hours.

Lemon-Herb Wild Turkey

YIELD: 7 (1-pint) jars | **PREP:** Active time, 15 minutes / Inactive time, 1 hour 35 minutes

The trick for this recipe is to only brown the outsides of the turkey, leaving the meat slightly undercooked. The remaining cooking process will take place during the pressure canning process while infusing the flavors from the lemon and fresh herbs.

3 tablespoons olive oil

8 pounds wild turkey

7 teaspoons salt

3 quarts water or poultry broth

2 whole lemons, sliced

2 whole lemons, zested and juiced

1 bunch fresh oregano, stemmed

1 bunch fresh thyme, stemmed

1. Heat a skillet or stockpot over medium-high heat. Once the skillet is hot, pour in the oil and heat until shimmering.

2. Season the turkey with the salt and add to the skillet, browning it in batches to avoid over-crowding the skillet, until slightly browned. The turkey should be slightly undercooked. Remove from the heat.

3. Heat a kettle with water until boiling. Remove from the heat.

4. Pack the turkey into jars, layering with the lemon slices, oregano, and thyme. Evenly portion the zest and juice and add on top of the turkey and lemon slices.

5. Cover the turkey with the broth, leaving 1 inch of headspace. Using the measurer, pop any air bubbles inside the jars and adjust the fill, if needed, to reach the proper headspace.

6. Dampen a corner of a paper towel with white vinegar and clean the jar rims. Place lids onto jars and, using a tea towel, lightly finger-tighten the bands onto the lids. Do not tighten past finger tight. Wipe jar rims to remove any oily residue.

7. Carefully lift the jars onto the rack in the canner without tilting the jars. Secure the lid onto the canner and heat the water to 140 degrees for Raw Pack recipes. Let the canner exhaust for 10 continuous minutes.

8. Place the pressure regulator or weighted gauge on the vent and process for 1 hour 15 minutes for pint jars in a dial gauge pressure canner at 11 pounds PSI or in a weighted gauge pressure canner at 10 pounds PSI.

9. Once completed, remove the canner from the heat. Carefully tilt the weight to make sure there is no more steam to escape before removing completely. Wait for 10 minutes, then carefully remove the lid.

10. Place the jars 1 inch apart on a clean towel, out of direct light, and leave undisturbed for at least 12 to 24 hours.

Ground Beef Three Ways

YIELD: 10 (1-pint) jars | **PREP:** Active time, 10 minutes / Inactive time, 1 hour 35 minutes

The recipe name says it all because it's perfect for maximizing time and creativity. Having jars of canned beef readily available in the pantry saves time in the kitchen. The beauty of preparing one protein multiple ways is that it's available to jump-start favorite recipes. Try using the ground beef in tomato juice for spaghetti or sloppy joes. Or try it in beef broth for tacos or chili and stews.

1 tablespoon olive oil
3 large yellow onions, diced
3 garlic cloves, minced
2 tablespoons salt
8 pounds ground beef
3 quarts water, beef broth, or tomato juice

1. Heat a large skillet over medium-high heat. Once the skillet is hot, pour in the oil and heat until shimmering. Add the onions and cook until they start to turn translucent, then add the garlic and salt and cook for 1 minute.

2. Add the ground beef and cook until browned. Remove from the heat.

3. Heat a kettle of water until boiling.

4. If using beef broth or tomato juice, heat until boiling, then remove from the heat.

5. Pack the ground beef into hot jars. Pour boiling water, broth, or tomato juice over the top, leaving 1 inch of headspace. Using the measurer, pop any air bubbles inside the jars and adjust the fill, if needed, to reach the proper headspace.

6. Dampen a corner of a paper towel with white vinegar and clean the jar rims. Place lids onto jars and, using a tea towel, lightly finger-tighten the bands onto the lids. Do not tighten past finger tight. Wipe jar rims to remove any oily residue.

7. Carefully lift the jars onto the rack in the canner without tilting the jars. Secure the lid onto the canner and heat the water to 180 degrees for Hot Pack recipes. Let the canner exhaust for 10 continuous minutes.

8. Place the pressure regulator or weighted gauge on the vent and process for 1 hour 15 minutes for pint jars in a dial gauge pressure canner at 11 pounds PSI or in a weighted gauge pressure canner at 10 pounds PSI.

9. Once completed, remove the canner from the heat. Carefully tilt the weight to make sure there is no more steam to escape before removing completely. Wait for 10 minutes, then carefully remove the lid.

10. Place the jars 1 inch apart on a clean towel, out of direct light, and leave undisturbed for at least 12 to 24 hours.

VARIATION TIP: Try substituting ground venison for the ground beef for a leaner version.

Beef Bone-In Short Ribs

YIELD: 8 (1-pint) jars | **PREP:** Active time, 1 hour / Inactive time, 1 hour 35 minutes

Beef bone-in short ribs are the epitome of savory. The pronounced beef flavor that comes from pressure canning these bone-in ribs is difficult to replicate. Try a homemade gravy to serve with the ribs.

3 tablespoons olive oil
4 pounds beef bone-in short ribs, cut to fit the size of the jars
½ teaspoon salt

1. Heat a skillet or stockpot over medium-high heat. Once the skillet is hot, pour in the oil and heat until shimmering.

2. Season the short ribs with the salt and add to the skillet, browning the ribs in batches to avoid overcrowding the skillet.

3. Heat a kettle of water until boiling. Remove from the heat.

4. Pack the browned short ribs into hot jars and pour boiling water over the top of the short ribs, leaving 1 inch of headspace. Using the measurer, pop any air bubbles inside the jars and adjust the fill, if needed, to reach the proper headspace.

5. Dampen a corner of a paper towel with white vinegar and clean the jar rims. Place lids onto jars and, using a tea towel, lightly finger-tighten the bands onto the lids. Do not tighten past finger tight. Wipe jar rims to remove any oily residue.

6. Carefully lift the jars onto the rack in the canner without tilting the jars. Secure the lid onto the canner and heat the water to 180 degrees for Hot Pack recipes. Let the canner exhaust for 10 continuous minutes.

7. Place the pressure regulator or weighted gauge on the vent and process for 1 hour 15 minutes for pint jars in a dial gauge pressure canner at 11 pounds PSI or in a weighted gauge pressure canner at 10 pounds PSI.

8. Once completed, remove the canner from the heat. Carefully tilt the weight to make sure there is no more steam to escape before removing completely. Wait for 10 minutes, then carefully remove the lid.

9. Place the jars 1 inch apart on a clean towel, out of direct light, and leave undisturbed for at least 12 to 24 hours.

Country-Style BBQ Pork Ribs

YIELD: 6 (1-pint) jars | **PREP:** Active time, 30 minutes / Inactive time, 1 hour 35 minutes

These country-style ribs are great served over garlic mashed potatoes or buttery white rice with a side of green beans. Or try the vegetable route and serve with asparagus, broccoli, or corn.

3 tablespoons olive oil

5 pounds boneless, country-style pork ribs

4 teaspoons salt

2 cups Sweet and Smoky Barbecue Sauce (see page 60)

3 quarts broth or water

1. Heat a skillet or stockpot over medium-high heat. Once the skillet is hot, pour in the oil and heat until shimmering.

2. Season the pork ribs with the salt and add to the skillet, browning the pork ribs in batches to avoid overcrowding the skillet. Remove from the heat.

3. In a small saucepan, combine the barbecue sauce and broth and bring to a boil. Remove from the heat.

4. Pack the browned pork ribs into hot jars and pour the barbecue sauce mixture over the top of the ribs, leaving 1 inch of headspace. Using the measurer, pop any air bubbles inside the jars and adjust the fill, if needed, to reach the proper headspace.

5. Dampen a corner of a paper towel with white vinegar and clean the jar rims. Place lids onto jars and, using a tea towel, lightly finger-tighten the bands onto the lids. Do not tighten past finger tight. Wipe jar rims to remove any oily residue.

6. Carefully lift the jars onto the rack in the canner without tilting the jars. Secure the lid onto the canner and heat the water to 180 degrees for Hot Pack recipes. Let the canner exhaust for 10 continuous minutes.

7. Place the pressure regulator or weighted gauge on the vent and process for 1 hour 15 minutes for pint jars in a dial gauge pressure canner at 11 pounds PSI or in a weighted gauge pressure canner at 10 pounds PSI.

8. Once completed, remove the canner from the heat. Carefully tilt the weight to make sure there is no more steam to escape before removing completely. Wait for 10 minutes, then carefully remove the lid.

9. Place the jars 1 inch apart on a clean towel, out of direct light, and leave undisturbed for at least 12 to 24 hours.

Spicy-Sweet Pork Bites

YIELD: 12 (1-pint) jars | **PREP:** Active time, 45 minutes / Inactive time, 1 hour 35 minutes

Few flavors go together as well as salty pork and sweet honey. These pork bites are irresistible and great for game day. Add a sampling of favorite cheeses to make an appetizer plate.

6 tablespoons olive oil

12 pounds pork shoulder, fat trimmed, cut into 1½-inch pieces

10 teaspoons salt

1 tablespoon freshly ground black pepper

1 tablespoon crushed red pepper flakes

1 cup honey

3 quarts water or broth

1. Heat a large stockpot over medium-high heat. Once the skillet is hot, pour in the oil and heat until shimmering.

2. Season the pork with the salt, pepper, and red pepper flakes, then add the pork to the skillet, browning in batches to avoid overcrowding the skillet.

3. Warm the honey until it can be easily poured, then coat the browned pork with the honey and toss. Remove from the heat.

4. Heat a kettle with water or broth until boiling. Remove from the heat.

5. Pack the pork bites into hot jars and top with the water or broth, leaving 1 inch of headspace. Using the measurer, pop any air bubbles inside the jars and adjust the fill, if needed, to reach the proper headspace.

6. Dampen a corner of a paper towel with white vinegar and clean the jar rims. Place lids onto jars and, using a tea towel, lightly finger-tighten the bands onto the lids. Do not tighten past finger tight. Wipe jar rims to remove any oily residue.

7. Carefully lift the jars onto the rack in the canner without tilting the jars. Secure the lid onto the canner and heat the water to 180 degrees for Hot Pack recipes. Let the canner exhaust for 10 continuous minutes.

8. Place the pressure regulator or weighted gauge on the vent and process for 1 hour 15 minutes for pint jars in a dial gauge pressure canner at 11 pounds PSI or in a weighted gauge pressure canner at 10 pounds PSI.

9. Once completed, remove the canner from the heat. Carefully tilt the weight to make sure there is no more steam to escape before removing completely. Wait for 10 minutes, then carefully remove the lid.

10. Place the jars 1 inch apart on a clean towel, out of direct light, and leave undisturbed for at least 12 to 24 hours.

Braised Lamb Neck

YIELD: 3 (1-quart) jars | **PREP:** Active time, 30 minutes / Inactive time, 1 hour 50 minutes

With this recipe, use bone-in lamb and then braise or pressure cook until tender. The flavor of the fat in the neck is mild and unmatched. A butcher should be able to help trim the neck.

6 tablespoons olive oil

8 pounds lamb neck, trimmed and cut crosswise

2 tablespoons salt

2 teaspoons freshly ground black pepper

1 large yellow onion, chopped

1 pint mushrooms, stemmed and chopped

3 carrots, and diced

3 celery stalks, diced

1 cup red wine

4 garlic cloves, smashed

1 (28-ounce) can crushed tomatoes

3 quarts water or broth

1. Heat a large stockpot over medium-high heat. Once the stockpot is hot, pour in the oil and heat until shimmering.

2. Season the lamb neck with the salt and pepper, then add to the stockpot, browning the neck in batches to avoid overcrowding the stockpot.

3. Add the onion, mushrooms, carrots, and celery and cook for 1 to 2 minutes, then add the wine, letting it cook for 1 to 2 minutes.

4. Add the garlic and crushed tomatoes, letting it cook for 1 to 2 minutes.

5. Cover with the broth and bring to a boil. Once boiling, reduce the heat and let simmer for 15 minutes, then remove from the heat.

6. Pack the lamb into hot jars and top with the broth from the stockpot, leaving 1 inch of headspace. Using the measurer, pop any air bubbles inside the jars and adjust the fill, if needed, to reach the proper headspace.

7. Dampen a corner of a paper towel with white vinegar and clean the jar rims. Place lids onto jars and, using a tea towel, lightly finger-tighten the bands onto the lids. Do not tighten past finger tight. Wipe jar rims to remove any oily residue.

8. Carefully lift the jars onto the rack in the canner without tilting the jars. Secure the lid onto the canner and heat the water to 180 degrees for Hot Pack recipes. Let the canner exhaust for 10 continuous minutes.

9. Place the pressure regulator or weighted gauge on the vent and process for 1 hour 30 minutes for quart jars in a dial gauge pressure canner at 11 pounds PSI or in a weighted gauge pressure canner at 10 pounds PSI.

10. Once completed, remove the canner from the heat. Carefully tilt the weight to make sure there is no more steam to escape before removing completely. Wait for 10 minutes, then carefully remove the lid.

11. Place the jars 1 inch apart on a clean towel, out of direct light, and leave undisturbed for at least 12 to 24 hours.

HOT PACK

Ground Venison Ragù

YIELD: 4 (1-pint) jars | **PREP:** Active time, 30 minutes / Inactive time, 1 hour 35 minutes

The best kind of ragù contains fat, so this recipe calls for adding 1 pound of ground pork to balance out the leanness of the venison.

2 carrots, cut into 1-inch pieces

1 medium white onion, quartered

1 celery stalk, ends trimmed and cut into 1-inch pieces

4 garlic cloves, peeled

4 to 6 tablespoons olive oil, divided

3 pounds ground venison

1 pound ground pork

1 teaspoon salt

½ teaspoon freshly ground black pepper

½ cup water or red wine

1. Put the carrots, onion, celery, and garlic in a food processor and process until almost smooth.

2. Heat a large stockpot over medium-high heat. Add 2 to 3 tablespoons of oil to the hot stockpot and heat until shimmering. Add the carrot, onion, and celery mixture, and cook until it starts to become fragrant.

3. If needed, add 2 to 3 more tablespoons of oil, then add the ground venison and pork to the stockpot. Season with the salt and pepper, then cook until mostly browned.

4. Add the water, cook for 1 to 2 minutes, then turn off the heat.

5. Portion the ragù into hot jars, leaving 1 inch of headspace. Using the measurer, pop any air bubbles inside the jars and adjust the fill, if needed, to reach the proper headspace.

6. Dampen a corner of a paper towel with white vinegar and clean the jar rims. Place lids onto jars and, using a tea towel, lightly finger-tighten the bands onto the lids. Do not tighten past finger tight. Wipe jar rims to remove any oily residue.

7. Carefully lift the jars onto the rack in the canner without tilting the jars. Secure the lid onto the canner and heat the water to 180 degrees for Hot Pack recipes. Let the canner exhaust for 10 continuous minutes.

8. Place the pressure regulator or weighted gauge on the vent and process for 1 hour 15 minutes for pint jars in a dial gauge pressure canner at 11 pounds PSI or in a weighted gauge pressure canner at 10 pounds PSI.

9. Once completed, remove the canner from the heat. Carefully tilt the weight to make sure there is no more steam to escape before removing completely. Wait for 10 minutes, then carefully remove the lid.

10. Place the jars 1 inch apart on a clean towel, out of direct light, and leave undisturbed for at least 12 to 24 hours.

RAW PACK

Elk Loin

YIELD: 12 (1-pint) jars | **PREP:** Active time, 30 minutes / Inactive time, 1 hour 35 minutes

Harvesting wild game is a great way to become self-sustaining while also providing a delicious and nutritious meat throughout the year. This recipe can be used for any red meat wild game or beef.

12 to 15 pounds elk meat, trimmed and cut into 1- to 1½-inch pieces

1 green bell pepper, stemmed, seeded, and thinly sliced

1 red bell pepper, stemmed, seeded, and thinly sliced

1 yellow onion, thinly sliced

1 teaspoon ground cumin

2 tablespoons salt

1 teaspoon ground paprika

2 teaspoons chili powder

1. In a bowl, combine the elk meat, green bell pepper, red bell pepper, and onion. Pack the pepper, onion, and meat mixture into jars, leaving 1 inch of headspace.

2. In a small bowl, combine the cumin, salt, paprika, and chili powder and add to the top of each full jar, dividing evenly.

3. Dampen a corner of a paper towel with white vinegar and clean the jar rims. Place lids onto jars and, using a tea towel, lightly finger-tighten the bands onto the lids. Do not tighten past finger tight. Wipe jar rims to remove any oily residue.

4. Carefully lift the jars onto the rack in the canner without tilting the jars. Secure the lid onto the canner and heat the water to 140 degrees for Raw Pack recipes. Let the canner exhaust for 10 continuous minutes.

5. Place the pressure regulator or weighted gauge on the vent and process for 1 hour 15 minutes for pint jars in a dial gauge pressure canner at 11 pounds PSI or in a weighted gauge pressure canner at 10 pounds PSI.

6. Once completed, remove the canner from the heat. Carefully tilt the weight to make sure there is no more steam to escape before removing completely. Wait for 10 minutes, then carefully remove the lid.

7. Place the jars 1 inch apart on a clean towel, out of direct light, and leave undisturbed for at least 12 to 24 hours.

VARIATION TIP: Cooking with wild game is a healthier alternative to beef. Wild game, like venison and elk, is much lower in fat and cholesterol and provides added benefits, as it is rich in omega-6 fatty acids.

Wild Hog Sausages

YIELD: 7 (1-quart) jars | **PREP:** Active time, 15 minutes / Inactive time, 1 hour 50 minutes

Panfry sliced sausages with peppers and onions and serve with garlic bread and a fresh salad. Try adapting this recipe by using pork sausage instead.

6 pounds raw linked sausages

1. Cut the linked sausages to fit to the necks of the jars, leaving 1 inch of headspace. Place the sausages in the jars; they should have room to move around slightly in the jars.

2. Dampen a corner of a paper towel with white vinegar and clean the jar rims. Place lids onto jars and, using a tea towel, lightly finger-tighten the bands onto the lids. Do not tighten past finger tight. Wipe jar rims to remove any oily residue.

3. Carefully lift the jars onto the rack in the canner without tilting the jars. Secure the lid onto the canner and heat the water to 140 degrees for Raw Pack recipes. Let the canner exhaust for 10 continuous minutes.

4. Place the pressure regulator or weighted gauge on the vent and process for 1 hour 30 minutes for quart jars in a dial gauge pressure canner at 11 pounds PSI or in a weighted gauge pressure canner at 10 pounds PSI.

5. Once completed, remove the canner from the heat. Carefully tilt the weight to make sure there is no more steam to escape before removing completely. Wait for 10 minutes, then carefully remove the lid.

6. Place the jars 1 inch apart on a clean towel, out of direct light, and leave undisturbed for at least 12 to 24 hours.

Sausage and Beef
Meatballs 124

Meals in a Jar

Chicken Cacciatore

YIELD: 8 (1-pint) jars | **PREP:** Active time, 30 minutes / Inactive time, 1 hour 35 minutes

"Cacciatore" means "hunter," so this meal is also known as hunter's chicken. It is a hearty chicken dish with onions, garlic, mushrooms, and herbs. Originating from central Italy, this meal is sure to satisfy.

3 tablespoons olive oil

3 pounds chicken tenderloins

1 tablespoon salt

1 teaspoon freshly ground black pepper

2 yellow onions, sliced

2 green bell peppers, stemmed, seeded, and sliced

¼ cup apple cider vinegar

2 pints Baby Bella mushrooms, sliced

4 garlic cloves, minced

28 ounces diced tomatoes with Italian herbs

2 teaspoons dried thyme

1. Heat a large stockpot over medium-high heat. Once hot, pour in the oil and heat until shimmering. Season the chicken with the salt and pepper. Start browning the chicken, for 2 to 3 minutes on each side. Remove the chicken to a plate and set aside.

2. Add the onions and bell peppers to the stockpot and cook for 3 to 4 minutes, or until they start getting tender. Deglaze the pot with the apple cider vinegar as needed. Remove the onions and peppers from the heat and add to the plate with the chicken.

3. Add the mushrooms to the stockpot and let them start to brown on each side. Add the chicken, onions, and bell peppers to the stockpot along with the mushrooms. Add the garlic, tomatoes, and thyme, then bring to a boil. Once boiling, reduce the heat and let simmer for 15 minutes. Remove from the heat.

4. Ladle the mixture into hot jars, leaving 1 inch of headspace. Using the measurer, pop any air bubbles inside the jars and adjust the fill, if needed, to reach the proper headspace.

5. Dampen a corner of a paper towel with white vinegar and clean the jar rims. Place lids onto jars and, using a tea towel, lightly finger-tighten the bands onto the lids. Do not tighten past finger tight. Wipe jar rims to remove any oily residue.

6. Carefully lift the jars onto the rack in the canner without tilting the jars. Secure the lid onto the canner and heat the water to 180 degrees for Hot Pack recipes. Let the canner exhaust for 10 continuous minutes.

7. Place the pressure regulator or weighted gauge on the vent and process for 1 hour 15 minutes for pint jars in a dial gauge pressure canner at 11 pounds PSI or in a weighted gauge pressure canner at 10 pounds PSI.

8. Once completed, remove the canner from the heat. Carefully tilt the weight to make sure there is no more steam to escape before removing completely. Wait for 10 minutes, then carefully remove the lid.

9. Place the jars 1 inch apart on a clean towel, out of direct light, and leave undisturbed for at least 12 to 24 hours.

Mango Chicken Curry

YIELD: 8 (1-pint) jars | **PREP:** Active time, 15 minutes / Inactive time, 1 hour 35 minutes

This curry is so delicious heated with a full-fat coconut milk or served alongside a long-grain white rice like basmati. Consider garnishing this curry with red pepper slices and cilantro.

1 tablespoon olive oil

1 large yellow onion, chopped

3 garlic cloves, chopped

1 knob ginger, cut into 1-inch pieces

2½ teaspoons salt

6 tablespoons yellow curry powder

8 pounds frozen mango pieces

3 pounds chicken breasts or thighs, cut into 1-inch pieces

1. Heat a large stockpot over medium-high heat. Once hot, pour in the oil and heat until shimmering.

2. Add the onion, garlic, and ginger and cook for 2 to 4 minutes, or until lightly browned. Add the salt and curry powder and cook for 1 minute. Add the mangos and 2 cups of water and cook for 1 minute. Remove from the heat.

3. Put the sautéed ingredients in a blender or food processor and process until mostly smooth.

4. Place the raw chicken pieces in jars, distributing evenly. Top the chicken with the mango mixture, leaving 1 inch of headspace. If needed, heat a kettle of water until boiling, then remove from the heat and top the jars with hot water to fill to 1 inch of headspace. Using the measurer, pop any air bubbles inside the jars and adjust the fill, if needed, to reach the proper headspace.

5. Dampen a corner of a paper towel with white vinegar and clean the jar rims. Place lids onto jars and, using a tea towel, lightly finger-tighten the bands onto the lids. Do not tighten past finger tight. Wipe jar rims to remove any oily residue.

6. Carefully lift the jars onto the rack in the canner without tilting the jars. Secure the lid onto the canner and heat the water to 140 degrees for Raw Pack recipes. Let the canner exhaust for 10 continuous minutes.

7. Place the pressure regulator or weighted gauge on the vent and process for 1 hour 15 minutes for pint jars in a dial gauge pressure canner at 11 pounds PSI or in a weighted gauge pressure canner at 10 pounds PSI.

8. Once completed, remove the canner from the heat. Carefully tilt the weight to make sure there is no more steam to escape before removing completely. Wait for 10 minutes, then carefully remove the lid.

9. Place the jars 1 inch apart on a clean towel, out of direct light, and leave undisturbed for at least 12 to 24 hours.

VARIATION TIP: Yellow curry is typically mild, so add red or green curry to turn up the heat.

RAW PACK

Sweet Paprika Chicken and Peppers

YIELD: 8 (1-pint) jars | **PREP:** Active time, 20 minutes / Inactive time, 1 hour 35 minutes

This recipe is inspired by Hungarian chicken paprikash, which gets its name from the sweet spice paprika. Serve this dish with dumplings, and add a spoonful of sour cream with a dash of fresh parsley to garnish.

28 ounces red bell peppers, stemmed and seeded

2 yellow onions, chopped

4 garlic cloves, peeled

½ cup sweet Hungarian paprika

1 tablespoon salt

3 quarts chicken broth or stock

4 pounds boneless, skinless chicken breasts, cut into 1-inch pieces

1. Put the bell peppers, onions, and garlic in a food processor and process until a chunky paste forms.

2. Heat a large stockpot over medium-high heat. Add the chunky paste, paprika, salt, and broth, then heat until boiling. Remove from the heat.

3. Portion the raw chicken into jars, distributing evenly, filling the jars three-fourths of the way to the top.

4. Ladle the hot liquid on top of the chicken, leaving 1 inch of headspace. Using the measurer, pop any air bubbles inside the jars and adjust the fill, if needed, to reach the proper headspace.

5. Dampen a corner of a paper towel with white vinegar and clean the jar rims. Place lids onto jars and, using a tea towel, lightly finger-tighten the bands onto the lids. Do not tighten past finger tight. Wipe jar rims to remove any oily residue.

6. Carefully lift the jars onto the rack in the canner without tilting the jars. Secure the lid onto the canner and heat the water to 140 degrees for Raw Pack recipes. Let the canner exhaust for 10 continuous minutes.

7. Place the pressure regulator or weighted gauge on the vent and process for 1 hour 15 minutes for pint jars in a dial gauge pressure canner at 11 pounds PSI or in a weighted gauge pressure canner at 10 pounds PSI.

8. Once completed, remove the canner from the heat. Carefully tilt the weight to make sure there is no more steam to escape before removing completely. Wait for 10 minutes, then carefully remove the lid.

9. Place the jars 1 inch apart on a clean towel, out of direct light, and leave undisturbed for at least 12 to 24 hours.

HOT PACK

Crustless Chicken Potpie

YIELD: 6 (1-pint) jars | **PREP:** Active time, 45 minutes / Inactive time, 1 hour 35 minutes

This recipe is a great place to use the Mirepoix recipe on page 38 by replacing the fresh onion, carrots, and celery with the preserved version. Serve this potpie by itself or with biscuits, or add to a flaky piecrust and bake for a satisfying family meal.

4 tablespoons olive oil, divided

2 large yellow onions, diced

2 cups thinly sliced carrots

2 cups thinly sliced celery

¼ cup dried Italian seasoning

4 garlic cloves, minced

3 tablespoons fresh parsley, chopped

4 teaspoons salt

1½ teaspoons freshly ground black pepper

2 cups potatoes, peeled and diced

4 quarts chicken broth or stock

2 cups frozen green peas

4 pounds boneless, skinless chicken breast, cut into 1-inch pieces

1. Heat a large stockpot over medium-high heat. Pour in 3 tablespoons of oil and heat until shimmering. Add the onions, carrots, celery, Italian seasoning, garlic, parsley, salt, and pepper and cook for about 10 minutes. Remove from the heat to a separate dish and set aside.

2. Add the remaining 1 tablespoon of oil to the stockpot and let it heat until shimmering. Add the potatoes and cook for about 10 minutes, or until they start to soften.

3. Add the broth, green peas, chicken, and onion mixture and bring to a boil over high heat. Once boiling, remove from the heat.

4. Ladle the mixture into hot jars, leaving 1 inch of headspace. Using the measurer, pop any air bubbles inside the jars and adjust the fill, if needed, to reach the proper headspace.

5. Dampen a corner of a paper towel with white vinegar and clean the jar rims. Place lids onto jars and, using a tea towel, lightly finger-tighten the bands onto the lids. Do not tighten past finger tight. Wipe jar rims to remove any oily residue.

6. Carefully lift the jars onto the rack in the canner without tilting the jars. Secure the lid onto the canner and heat the water to 180 degrees for Hot Pack recipes. Let the canner exhaust for 10 continuous minutes.

7. Place the pressure regulator or weighted gauge on the vent and process for 1 hour 15 minutes for pint jars in a dial gauge pressure canner at 11 pounds PSI or in a weighted gauge pressure canner at 10 pounds PSI.

8. Once completed, remove the canner from the heat. Carefully tilt the weight to make sure there is no more steam to escape before removing completely. Wait for 10 minutes, then carefully remove the lid.

9. Place the jars 1 inch apart on a clean towel, out of direct light, and leave undisturbed for at least 12 to 24 hours.

Pork Chile Verde

YIELD: 10 (1-pint) jars | **PREP:** Active time, 30 minutes / Inactive time, 1 hour 35 minutes

Serve this spicy pork stew with fresh cilantro, avocado, white onion, and lime wedges. Cool it down with a dollop of sour cream, and scoop it up with your favorite tortillas or corn chips.

3 tablespoons olive oil

4 pounds pork shoulder, fat trimmed, cut into 1-inch pieces

3½ teaspoons salt

2 tablespoons ground cumin

2 tablespoons dried oregano

3 large yellow onions, diced

2 jalapeño peppers, seeded and diced

3 garlic cloves, minced

14 ounces green chiles, diced

2 quarts chicken or beef stock or broth

1. Heat a large stockpot over medium-high heat. Once hot, pour in the oil and heat until shimmering. Season the pork with the salt, cumin, and oregano.

2. Add the pork to the stockpot and start browning, for 3 to 4 minutes on each side. Remove the pork to a plate and set aside.

3. Add the onions and jalapeños to the stockpot and cook for 3 to 4 minutes, or until they start turning translucent. Add the garlic and cook for 1 minute.

4. Add green chiles, pork, and stock to the stockpot, then bring to a boil. Once boiling, reduce the heat and let simmer for 15 minutes. Remove from the heat.

5. Ladle the stew into hot jars, leaving 1 inch of headspace. Using the measurer, pop any air bubbles inside the jars and adjust the fill, if needed, to reach the proper headspace.

6. Dampen a corner of a paper towel with white vinegar and clean the jar rims. Place lids onto jars and, using a tea towel, lightly finger-tighten the bands onto the lids. Do not tighten past finger tight. Wipe jar rims to remove any oily residue.

7. Carefully lift the jars onto the rack in the canner without tilting the jars. Secure the lid onto the canner and heat the water to 180 degrees for Hot Pack recipes. Let the canner exhaust for 10 continuous minutes.

8. Place the pressure regulator or weighted gauge on the vent and process for 1 hour 15 minutes for pint jars in a dial gauge pressure canner at 11 pounds PSI or in a weighted gauge pressure canner at 10 pounds PSI.

9. Once completed, remove the canner from the heat. Carefully tilt the weight to make sure there is no more steam to escape before removing completely. Wait for 10 minutes, then carefully remove the lid.

10. Place the jars 1 inch apart on a clean towel, out of direct light, and leave undisturbed for at least 12 to 24 hours.

Sausage and Beef Meatballs

YIELD: 8 (1-pint) jars | **PREP:** Active time, 45 minutes / Inactive time, 1 hour 35 minutes

Having meatballs on hand is convenient for a quick satisfying meal. A fantastic aspect of this recipe is the variety of options for mixing up the seasonings based on preference. Keep it simple, as this recipe calls for, then add seasonings and flavor when it comes time to heat up for dinner. Alternatively, divide the ground meat into separate bowls and season one for Italian-inspired meatballs, one for Swedish-style meatballs, and one for Greek-inspired meatballs.

1½ pounds ground beef

1½ pounds ground sausage

1 tablespoon onion powder

1 tablespoon garlic powder

2½ teaspoons salt

1 teaspoon freshly ground black pepper

1 tablespoon olive oil

3 quarts beef broth or stock

1. In a bowl, combine the ground beef and sausage with the onion powder, garlic powder, salt, and pepper. Using a tablespoon or cookie scoop, spoon enough of the ground beef mixture into your palm to form a 1- to 1½-inch meatball. Repeat until all the mixture has been used.

2. Heat a large stockpot over medium-high heat. Once hot, pour in the oil and heat until shimmering. Start browning the meatballs in a single layer until browned on each side, for 2 to 3 minutes. This will take several batches. Be sure not to overcrowd the stockpot to avoid steaming the meatballs. Set the browned meatballs to the side.

3. Heat a kettle with the broth until boiling. Remove from the heat.

4. Portion the browned meatballs into hot jars evenly. Cover the meatballs with the hot broth, leaving 1 inch of headspace. Using the measurer, pop any air bubbles inside the jars and adjust the fill, if needed, to reach the proper headspace.

5. Dampen a corner of a paper towel with white vinegar and clean the jar rims. Place lids onto jars and, using a tea towel, lightly finger-tighten the bands onto the lids. Do not tighten past finger tight. Wipe jar rims to remove any oily residue.

6. Carefully lift the jars onto the rack in the canner without tilting the jars. Secure the lid onto the canner and heat the water to 180 degrees for Hot Pack recipes. Let the canner exhaust for 10 continuous minutes.

7. Place the pressure regulator or weighted gauge on the vent and process for 1 hour 15 minutes for pint jars in a dial gauge pressure canner at 11 pounds PSI or in a weighted gauge pressure canner at 10 pounds PSI.

8. Once completed, remove the canner from the heat. Carefully tilt the weight to make sure there is no more steam to escape before removing completely. Wait for 10 minutes, then carefully remove the lid.

9. Place the jars 1 inch apart on a clean towel, out of direct light, and leave undisturbed for at least 12 to 24 hours.

Goulash

YIELD: 8 (1-pint) jars | **PREP:** Active time, 30 minutes / Inactive time, 1 hour 35 minutes

Goulash, or gulyás, is a traditional Hungarian stew that traces back to the 9th century and was a staple for European shepherds working the fields. The traditional recipe consisted of beef, onions, paprika, and tomatoes. This would be excellent served atop garlic mashed potatoes or noodles.

3 tablespoons olive oil

3 large yellow onions, chopped

3 large carrots, chopped

3½ pounds lean ground beef

1 tablespoon sweet Hungarian paprika

1 teaspoon onion powder

1 teaspoon garlic powder

3½ teaspoons salt

2 teaspoons freshly ground black pepper

28 ounces tomato sauce

1. Heat a large stockpot over medium-high heat. Once hot, pour in the olive oil and heat until shimmering. Add the onions and carrots and cook for 3 to 4 minutes.

2. Add the ground beef, paprika, onion powder, garlic powder, salt, and pepper, then cook for 5 to 7 minutes, or until it starts cooking through. Add the tomato sauce, cook for 1 minute, and remove from the heat.

3. Heat a kettle of water until boiling. Remove from the heat.

4. Portion the goulash into the hot jars evenly and top with the water, leaving 1 inch of headspace. Using the measurer, pop any air bubbles inside the jars and adjust the fill, if needed, to reach the proper headspace.

5. Dampen a corner of a paper towel with white vinegar and clean the jar rims. Place lids onto jars and, using a tea towel, lightly finger-tighten the bands onto the lids. Do not tighten past finger tight. Wipe jar rims to remove any oily residue.

6. Carefully lift the jars onto the rack in the canner without tilting the jars. Secure the lid onto the canner and heat the water to 180 degrees for Hot Pack recipes. Let the canner exhaust for 10 continuous minutes.

7. Place the pressure regulator or weighted gauge on the vent and process for 1 hour 15 minutes for pint jars in a dial gauge pressure canner at 11 pounds PSI or in a weighted gauge pressure canner at 10 pounds PSI.

8. Once completed, remove the canner from the heat. Carefully tilt the weight to make sure there is no more steam to escape before removing completely. Wait for 10 minutes, then carefully remove the lid.

9. Place the jars 1 inch apart on a clean towel, out of direct light, and leave undisturbed for at least 12 to 24 hours.

VARIATION TIP: Use chuck roast cut into 1-inch pieces or ground turkey instead of ground beef.

Italian Beef

YIELD: 8 (1-pint) jars | **PREP:** Active time, 10 minutes / Inactive time, 1 hour 35 minutes

Italian beef is delicious on soft hoagie rolls with provolone cheese. It's best when served as a hot, drippy beef bundle where the cheese gets all melty and the hoagie soaks up all the yummy juice. Alternatively, serve over roasted potatoes or cheesy grits for a tasty weeknight meal.

3 quarts water or beef broth

1 pound boneless beef short ribs, fat trimmed, cut into 2-inch pieces

1 pound sirloin or chuck roast, fat trimmed, cut into 2-inch pieces

16 ounces sliced pickled peperoncini, with juice

8 tablespoons Worcestershire sauce

2 pouches dry Italian dressing/marinade mix

1. Heat a kettle of water or beef broth until boiling. Remove from the heat.

2. Pack the raw beef pieces into jars, distributing the meat evenly and adding peperoncini slices throughout.

3. Add 1 tablespoon of peperoncini juice and 1 tablespoon of Worcestershire sauce to each jar. Top each jar with 1 tablespoon of dry Italian dressing and the boiling liquid, leaving 1 inch of headspace. Using the measurer, pop any air bubbles inside the jars and adjust the fill, if needed, to reach the proper headspace.

4. Dampen a corner of a paper towel with white vinegar and clean the jar rims. Place lids onto jars and, using a tea towel, lightly finger-tighten the bands onto the lids. Do not tighten past finger tight. Wipe jar rims to remove any oily residue.

5. Carefully lift the jars onto the rack in the canner without tilting the jars. Secure the lid onto the canner and heat the water to 140 degrees for Raw Pack recipes. Let the canner exhaust for 10 continuous minutes.

6. Place the pressure regulator or weighted gauge on the vent and process for 1 hour 15 minutes for pint jars in a dial gauge pressure canner at 11 pounds PSI or in a weighted gauge pressure canner at 10 pounds PSI.

7. Once completed, remove the canner from the heat. Carefully tilt the weight to make sure there is no more steam to escape before removing completely. Wait for 10 minutes, then carefully remove the lid.

8. Place the jars 1 inch apart on a clean towel, out of direct light, and leave undisturbed for at least 12 to 24 hours.

Sloppy Joes

YIELD: 8 (1-pint) jars | **PREP:** Active time, 30 minutes / Inactive time, 1 hour 35 minutes

Sloppy Joes are an easy, comforting meal to serve in a pinch. Simply butter sweet Hawaiian rolls and toast with melty cheddar cheese, and the family will be begging for more. To make this meal lighter, eat the sloppy Joes with a butterleaf lettuce salad, fresh tomatoes, and ranch dressing. Either way, it is sure to please.

4 pounds lean ground beef

4 teaspoons salt

2 teaspoons freshly ground black pepper

2 large yellow onions, diced

2 medium green bell peppers, stemmed, seeded, and diced

4 garlic cloves, minced

3 cups ketchup

2 cups water

¼ cup sugar

4 teaspoons chili powder

2 tablespoons hot sauce

1. Heat a large stockpot over medium-high heat. Once hot, put the ground beef in the pot, season with the salt and pepper, and cook until mostly browned. Remove the ground beef, set aside, and drain off most of the fat, leaving about 1 to 2 tablespoons.

2. Add the onions and bell peppers to the stockpot and cook for 2 to 3 minutes, or until they start to soften. Add the garlic and cook for 1 minute.

3. Add the ketchup, water, sugar, chili powder, and hot sauce and cook for 1 minute. Add the ground beef back to the stockpot with the rest of the ingredients and cook for 1 minute. Remove from the heat.

4. Portion the sloppy Joes into the hot jars, leaving 1 inch of headspace. Using the measurer, pop any air bubbles inside the jars and adjust the fill, if needed, to reach the proper headspace.

5. Dampen a corner of a paper towel with white vinegar and clean the jar rims. Place lids onto jars and, using a tea towel, lightly finger-tighten the bands onto the lids. Do not tighten past finger tight. Wipe jar rims to remove any oily residue.

6. Carefully lift the jars onto the rack in the canner without tilting the jars. Secure the lid onto the canner and heat the water to 180 degrees for Hot Pack recipes. Let the canner exhaust for 10 continuous minutes.

7. Place the pressure regulator or weighted gauge on the vent and process for 1 hour 15 minutes for pint jars in a dial gauge pressure canner at 11 pounds PSI or in a weighted gauge pressure canner at 10 pounds PSI.

8. Once completed, remove the canner from the heat. Carefully tilt the weight to make sure there is no more steam to escape before removing completely. Wait for 10 minutes, then carefully remove the lid.

9. Place the jars 1 inch apart on a clean towel, out of direct light, and leave undisturbed for at least 12 to 24 hours.

RAW PACK

Beef Stroganoff

YIELD: 8 (1-pint) jars | **PREP:** Active time, 5 minutes / Inactive time, 1 hour 35 minutes

Although dairy products should never be canned, this stroganoff can be canned sans sour cream, which you can add when serving. This creates a luxurious, creamy base that can be paired with your favorite noodles.

4 pounds beef chuck roast, fat trimmed, cut into 1-inch pieces

2 large yellow onions, sliced

2 pints Baby Bella mushrooms, sliced

6 ounces tomato paste

4 garlic cloves

3 tablespoons Dijon mustard

3 tablespoons Worcestershire sauce

3½ teaspoons salt

2 teaspoons freshly ground black pepper

3 quarts beef broth or stock

1. In a large bowl, combine the chuck roast, onions, mushrooms, tomato paste, garlic, mustard, Worcestershire sauce, salt, and pepper.

2. Heat the broth in a kettle until boiling. Remove from the heat.

3. Pack the chuck roast mixture into jars until three-fourths full, distributing evenly. Top the jars off with the hot broth, leaving 1 inch of headspace. Using the measurer, pop any air bubbles inside the jars and adjust the fill, if needed, to reach the proper headspace.

4. Dampen a corner of a paper towel with white vinegar and clean the jar rims. Place lids onto jars and, using a tea towel, lightly finger-tighten the bands onto the lids. Do not tighten past finger tight. Wipe jar rims to remove any oily residue.

5. Carefully lift the jars onto the rack in the canner without tilting the jars. Secure the lid onto the canner and heat the water to 140 degrees for Raw Pack recipes. Let the canner exhaust for 10 continuous minutes.

6. Place the pressure regulator or weighted gauge on the vent and process for 1 hour 15 minutes for pint jars in a dial gauge pressure canner at 11 pounds PSI or in a weighted gauge pressure canner at 10 pounds PSI.

7. Once completed, remove the canner from the heat. Carefully tilt the weight to make sure there is no more steam to escape before removing completely. Wait for 10 minutes, then carefully remove the lid.

8. Place the jars 1 inch apart on a clean towel, out of direct light, and leave undisturbed for at least 12 to 24 hours.

MEASUREMENT CONVERSIONS

VOLUME EQUIVALENTS	U.S. STANDARD	U.S. STANDARD (OUNCES)	METRIC (APPROXIMATE)
LIQUID	2 tablespoons	1 fl. oz.	30 mL
	¼ cup	2 fl. oz.	60 mL
	½ cup	4 fl. oz.	120 mL
	1 cup	8 fl. oz.	240 mL
	1½ cups	12 fl. oz.	355 mL
	2 cups or 1 pint	16 fl. oz.	475 mL
	4 cups or 1 quart	32 fl. oz.	1 L
	1 gallon	128 fl. oz.	4 L
DRY	⅛ teaspoon	–	0.5 mL
	¼ teaspoon	–	1 mL
	½ teaspoon	–	2 mL
	¾ teaspoon	–	4 mL
	1 teaspoon	–	5 mL
	1 tablespoon	–	15 mL
	¼ cup	–	59 mL
	⅓ cup	–	79 mL
	½ cup	–	118 mL
	⅔ cup	–	156 mL
	¾ cup	–	177 mL
	1 cup	–	235 mL
	2 cups or 1 pint	–	475 mL
	3 cups	–	700 mL
	4 cups or 1 quart	–	1 L
	½ gallon	–	2 L
	1 gallon	–	4 L

OVEN TEMPERATURES

FAHRENHEIT	CELSIUS (APPROXIMATE)
250°F	120°C
300°F	150°C
325°F	165°C
350°F	180°C
375°F	190°C
400°F	200°C
425°F	220°C
450°F	230°C

WEIGHT EQUIVALENTS

U.S. STANDARD	METRIC (APPROXIMATE)
½ ounce	15 g
1 ounce	30 g
2 ounces	60 g
4 ounces	115 g
8 ounces	225 g
12 ounces	340 g
16 ounces or 1 pound	455 g

ALTITUDE ADJUSTMENTS

PRESSURE CANNING ALTITUDE CHART		
Altitude in Feet	Dial-Gauge Canner	Weighted-Gauge Canner
0–1,000	10	10
1,001–2,000	11	15
2,001–4,000	12	15
4,001–6,000	13	15
6,001–8,000	14	15
8,001–10,000	15	15

RESOURCES

Amberoncini

amberoncini.com

My own small business featuring salts, blended seasonings, kitchen smallwares, and some of my favorite recipes I've created.

Ball Canning

BallMasonJars.com

I am a loyal Ball canner and appreciate the recipes, guides, and ideas Ball provides on this site.

Benson Knives

@benson.knife on Instagram

Aaron Benson makes the best custom knives on the planet, and I use them for all of my cooking.

The Canning Diva, Diane Devereaux

CanningDiva.com/contact/meet-the-diva

Diane is a fellow Rockridge Press author who has an excellent website stacked with recipes, resources, shopping, and a link to her podcast.

MeatEater

TheMeatEater.com

Steve Rinella is one of the greatest conservationists of our time. He is an avid hunter and cook. His site offers endless resources for hunting and preparing wild game.

National Center for Home Food Preservation

nchfp.uga.edu/publications/publications_usda.html#gsc.tab=0

A guide created by the USDA in 2009 and later revised in 2015 to assist those who were new to home canning. This is one of my favorite resources for all methods of canning and home food preservation.

REFERENCES

Devereaux, Diane, and Amber Day. *The Complete Guide to Pressure Canning.* Oakland, CA: Rockridge Press, 2021.

Home Food Preservation and Safety: Penn State Extension. Home Food Preservation and Safety | Penn State Extension. extension.psu.edu/food-safety-and-quality /home-food-safety.

Ingham, Barbara H, Steven C. Ingham, and Dennis R. Buege. *Canning Meat, Wild Game, Poultry & Fish Safely.* University of Wisconsin-Extension Cooperative Extension, 2002. foodsafety.wisc.edu/assets/pdf_Files/Canning%20Meat,%20Wild%20Game,%20 Poultry,%20&%20Fish%20Safely%20(B3345).pdf.

National Center for Home Food Preservation: UGA Publications. nchfp.uga.edu /publications/publications_usda.html#gsc.tab=0.

NIFA Staff. USDA's Complete Guide to Home Canning. National Institute of Food and Agriculture. nifa.usda.gov/about-nifa/blogs/usdas-complete-guide-home-canning.

Reynolds, Susan, and Paulette Williams. So Easy to Preserve. Bulletin 989. Cooperative Extension Service, the University of Georgia. Fifth Edition revised by Elizabeth Andress and Judy Harrison. 2006.

Schmutz, Pamela, and E. H. Hoyle. "Common Canning Problems." Home & Garden Information Center. Clemson College of Agriculture, Forestry and Life Sciences, March 20, 2012. hgic.clemson.edu/factsheet/common-canning-problems.

The USDA Complete Guide to Home Canning. Doublebit Press, 2020.

United States Department of Agriculture. *Complete Guide to Home Canning.* BN Publishing, 2009.

United States Department of Agriculture Food Safety and Inspection Service. "Clostridium botulinum & Botulism." Accessed January 2022. https://www.fsis.usda.gov /food-safety/foodborne-illness-and-disease/pathogens/clostridium-botulinum.

University of California, Division of Agriculture and Natural Resources. Publications: Methods. UC Master Food Preserver Program. mfp.ucanr.edu/Resources_ /Extension_Document_Library/Publications__Methods.

INDEX

About the Author

 **Amber Benson** is a cook, educator, and recipe developer originally from Oklahoma. Amber has lived across the country, including in Missouri, California, Washington, D.C., and Tennessee; she currently resides in Albuquerque, New Mexico. She has worked in the restaurant and food industry for twenty years and is most passionate about local growers, food systems, and eating delicious foods with incredible folks. She earned her bachelor's degree in business and organizational leadership and her master's in business administration. Amber has staged for James Beard Award–winning chefs, trained as a pitmaster in Houston, Texas, rolled burritos for a living, worked on an organic pear and cherry farm, earned her Master Food Preserver certification, and owns a custom blend spice business.